# CHICAGO'S GRAND HOTELS

### The Palmer House Hilton, The Drake, and The Hilton Chicago

# Chicago's Grand Hotels

## The Palmer House Hilton, The Drake, and The Hilton Chicago

Robert V. Allegrini

Published by Arcadia Publishing
Charleston SC, Chicago IL, Portsmouth NH, San Francisco CA

Printed in Great Britain

Library of Congress Catalog Card Number: 2005925969

For all general information contact Arcadia Publishing at:
Telephone 843-853-2070
Fax 843-853-0044
E-mail sales@arcadiapublishing.com
For customer service and orders:
Toll-Free 1-888-313-2665

Visit us on the Internet at http://www.arcadiapublishing.com

# CONTENTS

# ACKNOWLEDGMENTS

In attempting to present a combined total of nearly 300 years of hotel history it was necessary to obtain the assistance of many of my professional colleagues. Fortuitously for this author, it appears that it is simply in the nature of those engaged in the hospitality industry to be helpful. Therefore I would like to acknowledge the generous and capable support that I received from the following individuals who collectively have enabled this publication to be realized. First and foremost I would like to thank Hilton Hotels Corporation Senior Vice President of Operations, Central Division Ken Smith and Senior Vice President of Corporate Affairs Marc Grossman for their encouragement of this initiative. From The Palmer House Hilton I am grateful to Hilton Vice President and General Manager Gary Seibert, to Public Relations Director Ken Price, who is one of the foremost living authorities on The Palmer House, and to his kind assistant Nicolina Traverso. From The Drake I wish to express my gratitude to General Manager Gregor Andreewitch as well as to Marketing Assistant Ellen Cho and Executive Floor Manager Christine Folz. From The Hilton Chicago I desire to thank General Manager Tom Loughlin, Robert Neubert, director of Catering Operations and my former assistant, the current Public Relations Director of The Hilton Chicago Lynda Simonetti. Several other Hilton employees provided valuable assistance in this endeavor including Greg Jones and Amy Hulbert. Beyond those in the hospitality industry I wish to thank Tim Samuelson, the cultural historian for the Chicago Department of Cultural Affairs as well as Lois Weisberg, commissioner of the Chicago Department of Cultural Affairs. I also desire to thank my fiancée Cristina Bomben for her patience as I worked on this project for several months. Finally, I wish to thank legendary hotelier Richard Bayard, the "hotelier of kings and the king of hoteliers in the 21st century" for cultivating my passion for the subject of grand hotels.

*To Lida and the late Vincent Allegrini who had their first date in the Empire Room of The Palmer House and spent their wedding night at The Stevens.*

# INTRODUCTION

The grand hotel is truly a magical venue. It is a center of glamour, intrigue, and excitement, a place of romance and fascination. A place where all the ordinary rules of life are suspended a little bit, a place of indulgence.

Yet not just any large hotel can be classified as "grand." Most aficionados would agree that to earn the "grand" designation a hotel must possess an enticing combination of imposing and majestic architecture; rich, classical furnishings; unique function space; venerable dining establishments; and a legacy of both worldly and sophisticated hoteliers, as well as famous—and sometimes infamous—guests. Above all, a true grand hotel must possess a noteworthy history. It must be synonymous with the city where it is located.

Despite the many appealing characteristics of grand hotels, the forces of modern economics, changing tastes, and the march of time have all contributed to relegating these impressive edifices to the structural equivalent of the endangered species list.

Thankfully, Chicago has acted as a resilient refuge for these rare gems, and the city can boast three grand hotels that continue to flourish in the 21st century. The names of these hotels resonate with Chicagoans and discerning visitors of all ages: The Palmer House, The Drake, and The Hilton Chicago (which formerly bore the proud names of The Stevens and subsequently The Conrad Hilton). In the crowded pantheon of Chicago hotels, these three properties reign supreme not only because they have withstood the test of time but because so much of the most noteworthy and memorable social, cultural, and political history of the city has unfolded within their walls. Even the walls themselves have made history for

significant architectural and technological milestones are associated with the construction of each of these hotels. The second of the three Palmer Houses, for example, was the world's first completely fire proof hotel and was the first hotel to use electric light bulbs, to use an elevator, and to employ telephones in every room, and The Stevens, when opened, was simply the largest hotel in the world.

Big, brawny, and self-confident, The Palmer House, The Drake, and The Stevens reflected the city where they were built, and the era when they were born. As a convergence point of the railroads that crisscrossed the nation, Chicago in the late 1800s and early 1900s was a natural meeting place, and these three hotels emerged to accommodate the thousands of travelers who came to the city for business or social gatherings. The Drake, by virtue of its location on the shores of Lake Michigan, had the added advantage of attracting leisure travelers since it was positioned as one of America's first urban resorts. Today, few guests still arrive at The Palmer House, The Drake, or The Hilton Chicago by train. Though the modes of transportation have changed, the desirability of lodging at these hotels remains as strong as it did in the early decades of the last century. While sleeker more minimalist hotels that are often devoid of character or personality now dominate the urban landscape, The Palmer House, The Drake, and The Hilton Chicago continue to constitute enduring beacons for that cadre of cultured individuals who appreciate the finer things in life; who retain a sense of elegance; and who possess a desire to patronize a hotel where they can be a part of a tradition of gracious hospitality. The allure of Chicago's grand hotels continues and this is their story.

Potter Palmer was the builder and owner of The Palmer House and one of the true city fathers of Chicago. Beyond his legacy of the hotel that bares his name, Palmer was also responsible for beginning the dry goods store that eventually became Marshall Fields, as well as for literally making State Street that "great street" by buying nearly a mile of State Street real estate, having the thoroughfare widened by 27 feet, and literally turning the axis of mid town Chicago from east-west along a dingy Lake Street, to a more gracious north-south axis along State Street.

Bertha Honore Palmer was the great-granddaughter of Jean Antoine Honore, who had followed Lafayette to America. After her marriage to Potter Palmer she left several distinct legacies of her own to Chicago and the world. She was a pioneering champion of women's rights as well as a great patron of the arts. She amassed the greatest collection of impressionist art outside of France (over 220 paintings including numerous Monets and Renoirs) and willed them to the Art Institute of Chicago. To the delight of sweets' lovers everywhere, Bertha Palmer also earned a position in the annals of American culinary history through the creation of the brownie, which was first made in the kitchen of The Palmer House hotel to fulfill her request for a compact dessert that could be served at The Woman's Pavilion of the World's Columbian exhibition of 1892.

# ONE

# THE FIRST AND SECOND PALMER HOUSES

One is compelled to begin any history of The Palmer House by examining the colorful and larger than life figures of Potter and Bertha Palmer, the couple who gave their name to the hotels that they built and owned, and as such, earned an indelible place in the annals of Chicago history.

Potter Palmer was a dry goods merchant born in Potter's Hollow, New York, in 1826 who became intrigued with the business opportunities that the young city of Chicago offered and opened a dry goods store there in 1852 that eventually became the famed Marshall Field's department store. He became instantly famous for his here-to-fore unheard of business practices of allowing the return of goods for refund or exchange and offering bargain sales. With the considerable funds that he earned in the dry goods business he began speculating in Chicago real estate, and by the 1860s, he owned three-quarters of a mile of State Street in what is now the Loop.

Bertha Honore Palmer was born in Louisville, Kentucky, in 1849. She was the daughter of leading local businessman, Henry Honore, who later moved to Chicago with Bertha when she was six. She was 13 when she first met Potter Palmer, who was instantly taken with the beautiful young girl who was 23 years his junior. Potter patiently waited as Bertha continued her education. But when she turned 21, he could wait no longer, and they were married in the summer of 1871.

Potter Palmer planned to present the 225-room hotel he had just built as a wedding present to Bertha. But tragically, only 13 days after the hotel opened on September 26, 1871, the Great Chicago Fire reduced it, along with much of the rest of the city, to a heap of ashes. Undaunted by the loss of his entire real estate fortune, Potter Palmer immediately left for St. Louis and negotiated a loan on his signature only for $1.7 million, which was believed to be the largest individual loan ever recorded to that date. He began reconstructing his many properties and among them his most enthusiastic endeavor—the rebuilding of The Palmer House.

Choosing a site across the street from the original Palmer House, he began construction on the second Palmer House. Less than a year later, in July of 1873, it was opened to the public amidst much fanfare of being the first truly fireproof hotel in the world. This impressive new structure was eight stories tall, which was unheard of for hotels of the period because of the need to transport luggage and guests via stairs. Palmer solved the problem by installing a "perpendicular railroad" to "connect floor with floor, rendering passage by the stairs unnecessary." Hence the elevator was born into public service.

The second Palmer House soon became one of the social centers of Chicago. The hotel's bar room, featuring an 85-foot bar, became the city's preferred drinking venue, and the hotel's dining room was amongst Chicago's most opulent. The growing reputation of The Palmer House enabled it to boast a very prestigious guest list. In 1880, James Garfield, the Republican nominee for president, held an impromptu reception on the grand staircase in the lobby as 1,000 people milled by, shaking his hand. In 1884, Pres. Grover Cleveland carried on the staircase tradition, only playing to a much larger audience.

The Palmer House also became the location of many important historic events. In 1879, less than two years after the massacre of General Custer and the 7th Cavalry at the Battle of the Little Bighorn, the formal inquiry into cause of the debacle was held at The Palmer House. Known as the Reno Court of Inquiry, the event took its name from Custer's surviving colleague Maj. Marcus Reno, who was absolved of any guilt at the proceedings. Also in 1879, one of the 19th century's most celebrated banquets was held in the second Palmer House when Gen. Ulysses S. Grant returned from a world trip and was feted by the likes of General Sherman and Mark Twain.

During the heyday of the second Palmer House in the late 19th century, the Palmers earned the status as one of Chicago's leading couples. They enjoyed great wealth but were also noteworthy philanthropists. Palmer Potter died on May 4, 1902, leaving a large fortune to Bertha. An extremely savvy business woman in her own right, Bertha was able to double Potter's fortune principally by being a pioneer investor in Sarasota, Florida, real estate. She continued to run the second Palmer House, but by the second decade of the 20th century, the hotel was clearly dated. Bertha began to advance plans to build a third Palmer House on the same sight as the existing Palmer House, which now was an extremely valuable piece of Chicago real estate. Sadly, Bertha Palmer died in 1918, unable to see the realization of the dream of a new Palmer House. However, her vision of a magnificent hotel, done in an opulent French style, which paid homage to her own French heritage and Francophile tastes, had already been set in motion. Soon a third Palmer House would be born.

THE OLD PALMER HOUSE BEFORE THE FIRE.

The original 1871 Palmer House that stood at the northwest corner of State and Quincy was intended as a wedding present from Potter Palmer to Bertha. The structure cost $200,000 to construct and an additional $100,000 to furnish. The hotel was inaugurated on September 26, 1871, and operated for only 13 days before the Great Chicago Fire caused it to burn to the ground. Undeterred by this tragedy, Palmer resolved to build a new and better Palmer House.

This advertisement announced the opening of the second Palmer House. As the advertisement demonstrates, Palmer was fond of using superlatives to describe his new hotel and its amenities, such as "The Largest and Best Furnished Hotel in the World," "The Palace Hotel of the World," the "Finest Restaurant in the City," and last but certainly not least, given the history of the previous Palmer House, the "Only fire-proof House in the United States."

The second Palmer House was built across the street from the original Palmer House on the site of the current Palmer House (State and Monroe). It opened on November 8, 1873, and stood for more than 50 years before it was razed in two sections as the current Palmer House was being conversely erected in two sections between 1924 and 1927 on the same site. As such, guests were simply relocated from the old to the new sections as construction continued. Therefore, the hotel never officially closed, allowing The Palmer House to boast that it is the oldest hotel in continual operation in the United States currently at 132 years. Note that, in an early example of graphic manipulation, this interesting photograph of The Palmer House exterior has been embellished with a cartoon like foreground that includes automobiles, which was probably done to make the photograph appear more "modern."

This is the Grand Hall and Rotunda of the second Palmer House. The hotel was considered so opulent for its time that Oscar Hammerstein actually set the second act of the musical *Show Boat* in The Palmer House of 1899 to convey an immediately recognizable sense of wealth and high style for his characters Gaylord and Magnolia Ravenal, who lived at the hotel "when times were good." The Palmer House of that period actually had many permanent residents.

The bar room of the second Palmer House became one of the legendary drinking establishments in pre-prohibition Chicago. One of the attractions was the bar that extended a full 85 feet. Another attraction was an adjoining billiard room where guests could watch championship billiard contests.

Seen here is the "Dining Hall" of The Palmer House. The Palmer House was the sight of many fabled epicurean events, including the 1879 banquet in honor of the return of Gen. Ulysses S. Grant from a two-year around the world trip. At the culmination of this banquet, which featured 500 dignitaries eating, drinking, and listening to oratory for over six hours, Mark Twain, who served as the dinner's master of ceremonies, jumped on a table at approximately 2:00 a.m. and gave a speech that, in Twain's own words, "shook him [Grant] up like dynamite" and caused the general to "laugh and cry like the mortalest of mortals."

The flamboyant Potter Palmer knew that some of the wealthiest and most influential men in the nation would be patronizing the barber shop of The Palmer House. So, to make sure these individuals realized that he, too, was a man of wealth and stature, Palmer had the floor of the barbershop paved with over $300 in U.S. silver dollars. As the coins wore through, approximately every three years, they were replaced. The custom had to be discontinued when it became illegal to deface United States currency.

This Palmer House menu cover dates to November 27, 1884. The Palmer House offered guests the opportunity to participate in either the "American" or "European Plans." In the American Plan, meals were included in the room rate, and in the European Plan, meals were separate.

Amongst the many treasures of The Palmer House is Mrs. Palmer's beloved French Havilland bone china, which she acquired on one of her several trips to Europe and which was used for special occasions at the hotel during the late 19th century. Each piece of each place setting is trimmed in pure 24-karat gold. One setting was comprised of 16 separate pieces. Today each setting is valued at approximately $6,800.

# PALMER HOUSE GENTLEMEN'S CAFE
## ·DINNER·

Souvenir Menu from
Saturday, June 5, 1909
THE PALMER HOUSE, CHICAGO
From 12 M. to 3 P. M. and 5:30 P. M. to 7:30 P. M.

Blue Points............. 20    Little Neck Clams.. 20

### SOUP
Cream of Asparagus......... 15    Italian Paste...... ............. 15

### FISH
Baked Red Snapper, Wine Sauce.............. 25
Parisian Potatoes

### BOILED
Brisket of Beef, Horseradish Sauce............ 25

### ROAST
Beef ........................... 30    Turkey, Cranberry Sauce.. 40
Loin of Pork, Apple Sauce...... 25

Broiled Quail on Toast ...... 40    Broiled Plover on Toast.... 30

### ENTREES
Breast of Lamb Breaded, with Peas ...................... 30
Fried Frog Legs, Tomato Sauce................................ 30
Rice Fritters, Vanilla Flavor..................................... 15
Baked Pork and Beans................ 20

### COLD
Lobster Salad.................... 30    Sliced Cucumbers............ 15
Salmon Mayonnaise........... 25    Celery ....................... 10
Spiced Oysters.................... 25    Dill Pickles.................. 5
Roast Beef ... 30; with Potato Salad 40    Pickled Beets...... 5
Roast Chicken or Lamb with Lettuce or Potato Salad....... 40
Lettuce or Chicory Salad... 20    Melon Mangoes .............. 10
Boiled Lobster, with Chow-chow or Chili Sauce...... 40

### VEGETABLES
Mashed or Boiled Potatoes 5    Baked Sweet Potatoes...... 5
Hubbard Squash........ ...... 5    Wax Beans................. 5
Boiled Onions.................. 5    Hulled Corn.................. 5

### DESSERT
English Plum Pudding, Hard and Brandy Sauce..... 10
Apple Pie........................ 10    Mince Pie...................... 10
Cherry Pie ...... ............. 10    Lemon Custard Pie............ 10
Pies with Ice Cream......... 15    Peach Pie.................... 10
Benedictine Punch........... 10    Palmer House Ice Cream.... 10
Assorted Cakes............... 10

### FRUIT
Oranges 10    Apples 10    Pears 15    Bananas 10    Grapes 15
Assorted Fruit .......... 25

American, Edam, Brie or Caprera Cheese and Cracker 10
Coffee with Cream........... 10    Small Cup Black Coffee...... 5

Bass' Ale from the wood, 10c. per mug.
Ye Old Musty Ale, 10c. per mug.

**Restaurant for Ladies and Gentlemen on Parlor Floor**
**The Drinking Water is Boiled and Filtered.**

Palmer House, Ladies' Entrance, 1903

Separation of the sexes at The Palmer House was evident, as the juxtaposition of items on this page attest. The menu above is from the "Gentleman's Café," which was the exclusive purview of men. Note at the conclusion of the menu that patrons were reassured that "drinking water is boiled and filtered." It is also interesting to note that the midwestern penchant for early dining is already evident from this 1909 menu, which lists the café's hours of operation between only 5:30 and 7:30 p.m.

This 1903 photograph shows the ladies entrance to The Palmer House. At the time it was not uncommon for hotels to have ladies entrances for use by unescorted female guests. The entrance offered legitimate lady guests an opportunity to arrive at the hotel without the fear of encountering unwanted male attention, and it also offered hotel management the opportunity to control the comings and goings of "ladies of the evening." This portion of the hotel bearing the date of 1872 was completed before the remainder of the hotel, which opened in 1873.

This view of the second Palmer House looks west down Monroe Street during the bustling years of the early 1900s. During this period, the Hotel DeJonghe stood opposite The Palmer House. Note the sign on the balcony opposite The Palmer House. It was here where Shrimp DeJonghe was invented. Today the sight is the Carson Pirie Scott department store.

126—Palmer House, Chicago

The famous lobby of the current Palmer House is seen here with its Tiffany 24-karat gold-sheathed chandeliers blazing at the entrance of the Empire Room and its magnificent, painted ceiling by the distinguished French artist Louis Pierre Rigal. In a 1995 article on The Palmer House, the *Chicago Tribune* referred to The Palmer House lobby as one of Chicago's "most popular and picturesque meeting places" and went on to state that the lobby has long been "beckoning those who call Chicago home and those who consider it a home away from home."

# TWO

The Third and current Palmer House looked radically different than its predecessor as evidenced by this post card that was produced shortly after the completion of the hotel in 1927. It was built at a cost of $20 million and furnished for an additional $20 million. The building rose to 24 stories and contained 2,268 guest rooms all with their own baths. For a very short time it held the distinction of being the largest hotel in the world before it was eclipsed by The Stevens which opened later in 1927.

# THE THIRD AND CURRENT PALMER HOUSE

By the time Potter Palmer Jr. laid the cornerstone for the current Palmer House on June 3, 1925, it was already "the Chicago hotel the world knows best," to borrow a phrase from the hotel's current publicity. During more than half a century in operation, the fame of the second Palmer House had spread far and wide, so there was much interest in every aspect of the forthcoming structure when plans for the project were first announced to the public in 1923. For example, upon learning of the manner in which the new Palmer House would be furnished, *Hotel Monthly* magazine, which was closely monitoring developments reported, "The contract for the purchase of furniture has been awarded to Carson, Pirie, Scott & Company, whose expert experience backed by sufficient funds to buy the best of everything, is expected to result in the Palmer House being in many respects the best furnished hotel in the world."

There was also a great deal of interest in the innovative plans put forth by the architectural firm of Holabird and Roche to raze half of the old hotel and build half of the new hotel, while keeping the remaining half of the old hotel open for business. As such, the first phase of the new building, containing the main lobby, Empire Dining Room, and Grand Ballroom, was completed on December 24, 1925. When this section was complete, guests from the remaining half of the old hotel were simply transferred before it was razed, and construction begun on the second half of the new hotel, which was finished in 1927. In this matter, the hotel could claim to have remained open while an entirely new structure was built on the same plot of land.

Once opened, the third Palmer House added to the illustrious reputation of its predecessors. Its outstanding location in the heart of Chicago's burgeoning Loop enabled the hotel's six dining venues to thrive. Even the Great Depression, which eventually caused The Drake and The Stevens to teeter, could not stop The Palmer House. In fact, in 1933, during the height of the Great Depression, The Palmer House began the transformation of the Empire Dining Room into the famous supper club, which supported big name entertainment for the next four decades.

The success of The Palmer House did not escape Conrad Hilton, who was busy building his empire in the 1930s and early 1940s. He had always liked Chicago. In his autobiography, *Be My Guest*, Conrad Hilton states "Chicago had charms," and he recalls being in Chicago during his honeymoon trip and making the following statement to his wife: "'Some day,' I told Mary, 'I'm going to come back and find a vacant lot. I'd like to build me a hotel here.'" That "someday" was to occur in 1945, but it was The Stevens and not the Palmer House that first interested Hilton. Out of frustration over his seeming lack of success in striking a deal with the then owner of The Stevens, Stephen Heally, Hilton approached the Palmer Estate, which still owned The Palmer House and began negotiations to purchase that property for $19,385,000. In the meantime, Heally acquiesced, and Hilton wound up with The Stevens as well, giving him two of Chicago's grand hotels.

Subsequent to Hilton's acquisition of The Palmer House, the hotel continued to serve as a focal point of Chicago's social life particularly as a result of the Empire Room, which now had the reputation of being one of the leading supper clubs in the nation.

The hotel was able to weather the vicissitudes of State Street during the 1960s and 1970s when the long established "great street" lost its shopping preeminence to North Michigan Avenue. Much like with the second Palmer House a century earlier, a new downtown grew up around the third Palmer House in the 1980s and 1990s. The revitalization of the nearby theater district during this period gave The Palmer House an added boost and enabled the hotel to become extremely successful in the marketing of theater packages.

Famed guests from around the world also continue to frequent The Palmer House. One of the largest gatherings of such international luminaries occurred in 1993 when the hotel hosted the second Parliament of World Religions. This event saw major religious figures from the Dali Lama to Bishop Desmond Tutu register as guests of the hotel. Representatives of over 90 different religions were present at the weeklong conference, including a coven of practicing witches! The first Parliament of World Religions was held at the previous Palmer House a century earlier during the Columbian Exhibition of 1893.

Today, more than 130 years after Potter Palmer conceived of a grand hotel on the squalid mud road that was State Street and had the city built around it, The Palmer House can legitimately lay claim to the title of the oldest, continually operating hotel in North America. It is an honor that Chicagoans cherish, for the hotel has come to symbolize both the city's rebirth after the Great Fire and its continued dominance as the center of the nation's meetings and conventions.

The opulent French Empire décor of the public space of the current Palmer House is evident from this photograph of a banquet of the National Retail Luggage Dealers Association taken in the "Colonnade Foyer" of the Grand Ballroom in 1927. The foyer, which today is known as the State Ballroom, is a space that opens onto the Grand Ballroom. Its clever design allows the space to serve as a stand alone ballroom for smaller functions as well as serving as pre-function space for events in the Grand Ballroom, and given its view directly into the Grand Ballroom, as a venue capable of extending the seating capacity of the Grand Ballroom.

This rare "back of the house" photograph shows some of the 1,200 employees it took to run The Palmer House in the 1920s. "Back of the house" is a hospitality expression used to describe those areas of the hotel that are for employees only. Here gentlemen are working behind the hotel's front desk. Note the rack between the windows. Prior to the era of computer automation, the status of the guest rooms in hotels were kept on cards that were filed in such racks. Each guest room had its own rack space. Hence the hospitality expression "rack rate" for the "full published rate" of a room that was printed on the room's rack card.

THIRD ANNUAL FORMAL SUPPER DANCE
CATERING EXECUTIVES CLUB OF AMERICA
PALMER HOUSE     CHICAGO     FEBRUARY 22, 1937

The Grand Ballroom of the current Palmer House is packed for the third annual formal supper dance of the Catering Executives Club of Chicago dating to February 22, 1937. This organization is still very much in existence today. Throughout the late 1920s, 1930s, and 1940s the Grand Ballroom of The Palmer House hosted some of Chicago's most elegant and important gala events. According to Holabird and Roche, the architectural firm responsible for the hotel, the Grand Ballroom "displays the restrained and monumental character of the period of Louis the XVI."

NORWEGIAN AMERICAN COMMITTEE OF CHICAGO
DINNER IN HONOR OF HIS ROYAL HIGHNESS
CROWN PRINCE OLAV OF NORWAY
AND HER ROYAL HIGHNESS
CROWN PRINCESS MARTHA OF NORWAY
PALMER HOUSE CHICAGO MAY 5, 1939

In May of 1939, on the eve of the Second World War, Chicago was visited by Crown Prince Olav and Crown Princess Martha of Norway, and a gala dinner was held in their honor in the Grand Ballroom of The Palmer House. Note the balcony seating, which increased the capacity of the ballroom by a quarter.

When the current Palmer House was completed, it boasted six dining rooms, including the Empire Room, the Victorian Room, the Chicago Room, the Petit Café, the Main Café and Yellow Room, and the Coffee Shop. The most formal of these dining rooms were the Victorian Room, seen above, which was designed to remind guests of the style of the previous Palmer House and the Empire Room pictured at left. The Empire Room, like much of the rest of the current Palmer House, was French inspired and named in homage to French Emperor Napoleon and his beloved Josephine.

On the more casual end of the dining spectrum, The Palmer House of the 1930s could boast Le Petit Café, which was billed in advertising as the most famous café in the Middle West. The Petit Café lasted until late 1960s when the space was transformed into another food and beverage outlet known as the Den.

The Coffee Shop, also originally known as the Lunch Room, featured a seemingly never-ending serpentine counter. By the 1940s, this extremely popular restaurant located on the hotel's lower level was primarily used as a breakfast venue. It subsequently opened again for lunch and was the home of the famous Palmer House style Dover sole, which was the most requested item on the menu of the hotel for decades. It was referred to as "Palmer House style" because it was in fact not Dover sole but actually halibut. The Coffee Shop survived until 1985 when it was transformed into a restaurant called "Boca Raton." In 1991, it was subsequently re-baptized as the Coffee Shop. However, this incarnation of the Coffee Shop lasted only four years before closing in 1995.

On the occasion of Chicago's Century of Progress Exhibition in 1933, the Empire Room, which had opened as the hotel's principal dining room in 1925 (upon the completion of the first half of the third Palmer House), began its tradition of serving as a supper club and featuring big name entertainment. Here Maurice Chevalier performs. During the more than four decades that the Empire Room served as a supper club, it played host to numerous stars, including the likes of Frank Sinatra, Tony Bennett, Ethel Merman, Ella Fitzgerald, Hildegarde, Sophie Tucker, Harry Belafonte, Celeste Holm, Sid Caesar, Eartha Kitt, Danny Kaye, Andy Williams, George Burns, Milton Berle, and Bob Newhart.

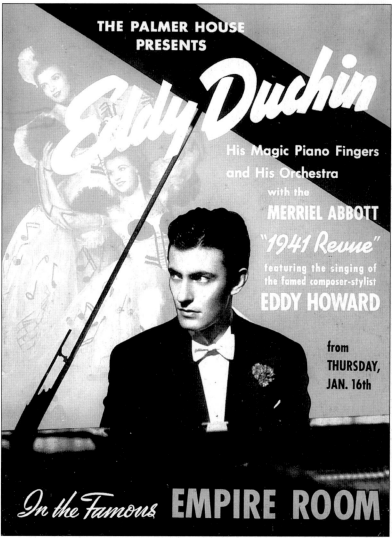

The Empire Room also had a reputation for launching virtual unknowns. The great Bob Fosse began dancing there in his early twenties, and following World War II, a young man from Milwaukee was hired to play cocktail music as guests were being seated. His name was Lee Liberace. As is evidenced by the advertisement above, patrons had to learn how to pronounce his name!

Eddie Duchin was another pianist who performed with his "magic fingers" at The Palmer House. Most of the shows at the Empire Room were produced and booked by entertainment impresario Merriel Abbott, whose name appears on this program. Abbott was one of the first female executives hired by Conrad Hilton. She was a former dancer who had her own dance studio. Hilton originally hired her as a choreographer, but her role soon expanded to the booking of big name talent for the Empire Room.

Chicago's answer to the Rockettes were the Abbott Dancers. Named for producer and choreographer Merriel Abbott, the dancers performed at the Empire Room from the 1930s though the 1960s. Abbott proved to be a tough guardian for the dancers, who were compelled to participate in a weigh-in each Thursday and who were supposedly forbidden from dating any of the orchestra players because she felt they were "unreliable."

When big name acts were not playing in the Empire Room, it was often used for prestigious special events. Here, in this photograph, which clearly shows the Empire Room in all of its glory, the 1958 Ms. Chicago Pageant was held in the venue.

In the 1950s and 1960s, the Empire Room reigned supreme as the premiere supper club in the city of Chicago. Amongst the perennial favorite performers was Jimmy Durante, who made several appearances at the Empire Room. Here, the legendary "Schnoz," as he was affectionately known, receives a standing ovation from the audience.

Jimmy Durante returned to the Empire Room along with Carol Channing for the 100th anniversary of The Palmer House in 1971. Here, they appear dressed as Potter and Bertha Palmer. Channing was one of the most prolific performers at the Empire Room, appearing there twice a year for over 20 years.

Two views of the Empire Room show how crowded the venue was in its prime when it accommodated its maximum capacity of 250 guests. In 1954, the beautiful crystal and gold chandeliers that appear in both of these photographs were sold to a salvage dealer for $400 each for the sake of modernization. Conrad Hilton was so incensed by their removal that the hotel was compelled to subsequently buy them back at a cost of $4,000 each!

### APPETIZERS

Cocktail Sauce or Mignonette Sauce (10c. extra)

| | | | |
|---|---|---|---|
| Blue Points . . . . . . . . . 50 | Rockaways . . . . . . . . . 60 |
| Cherrystones . . . . . . . . 50 | Little Necks . . . . . . . . 45 |
| Lobster Cocktail . . . . . 1.50 | Shrimp Cocktail . . . . . . 75 |
| Clam Juice Cocktail Frappe .60 | Supreme of Fruit . . . . . . 50 |
| Tomato Juice . . . . . . . .30 | Hors-d'Oeuvres, Bellevue . .90 |

Smoked Nova Scotia Salmon 1.25

### SOUPS

| | |
|---|---|
| Clam Chowder . . . . . . . 40 | *Potage Palmer House . . . . 50 |
| Chicken Broth . . . . . . . 35 | *Palmer House Clam Chowder 40 |
| Jellied Consomme . . . . . 45 | *Cold Palmeroise . . . . . . 50 |

### A LA CARTE SPECIALS

Roast Leg of Lamb, Mint Jelly 1.50
*Roast Young Tom Turkey, Cranberry Sauce 1.50

**COLD SALMON BELLEVUE**
From the Columbia River,
Poached in White Wine and
served with our Special
Tarragon Dressing
One Dollar Thirty-five Cents

**\*SUPREME OF CHICKEN, MONROE**
Breast of Chicken and Mushrooms
Sauted, finished in White Wine
Sauce, Cream, Hollandaise and
Tomato Catsup, served on Toast
Two Dollars

### FRESH VEGETABLES

Cooked to order in Pressure Cooking Vessels

*Vegetarian Dinner . . . . . . . . . . . . . . . . . .1.00
Peas, Garden Spinach, String Beans, Broccoli or Brussels Sprouts . .45
Potatoes Baked (to order) 35; Mashed or Boiled . . . . . . .30

### SALADS

| | |
|---|---|
| *Palmer House Fruit Salad . .65 | French Salad Bowl . . . . .50 |
| Chef's Salad . . . . . . . .50 | Tomato . . . . . . . . . .45 |
| Lettuce . . . . . . . . . .40 | Belgian Endive . . . . . .45 |

"In addition to the amount quoted, an amount equal to two per cent (2%), representing additional expense occasioned by the Illinois Retailers Occupational Tax Act will be added as a separate item in determining the aggregate price of your purchase."

---

## Empire Dinner

### THREE DOLLARS

Plus 20% U. S. Cabaret Tax

This Dinner Served until 10:00 P. M.

*Indicates Palmer House Specialties
Butter—Only One Piece to a Person

| | |
|---|---|
| Cold Soups | Tomato Juice |
| Clam Juice Frappe | Seafood Cocktail |

Chopped Chicken Liver Canape

| | |
|---|---|
| Clam Chowder | Chicken Broth |

*Palmer House Celery and California Olives

*Baked Stuffed Lake Superior Whitefish Palmer House
Fried Frog Legs, Cold Egg Sauce
Stewed Oysters, Mariniere
Curried Fresh Gulf Shrimps, Benares
Half Lobster any Style—One Dollar Additional
Fricassee of Spring Chicken Jardiniere
Breaded Mignon of Veal Milanaise
Braised Leg of Lamb, Chipolata
Broiled Fresh Mushrooms with Canadian Bacon, Colbert Butter
*Roast Young Tom Turkey, Cranberry Sauce
Fresh Vegetable Dinner with Braised Celery and Poached Egg
Cold Shrimps and Lobster Salad in Shell Ravigotte
Cold Roast Capon and Smoked Beef Tongue, Spiced Pears

*Palmer House Rolls and Butter

| | |
|---|---|
| Carrots and Peas Fines Herbes | Parsley Potato |

Mixed Green Salad

*Palmer House Apple Pie

| | |
|---|---|
| Rum Pie | Home-made Cheese Cake |
| Fig Custard Pudding, Port Wine Sauce | Banana Jell-o Delight |
| Tutti Frutti Ice Cream | *Frozen Ice Cream Slice |
| *Palmer House Chocolate Ice Cream | Delicious Apple |

Cream Cheese with Toasted Crackers

Coffee

**CABARET TAX**
The new Federal Revenue Act requires a 20 per cent "Cabaret Tax", effective July 1, 1944, in all public rooms where entertainment or dancing is provided. The "Cabaret Tax" applies to all food and beverage items.
Minimum Dinner Check (until 10 P. M.) $3.00; Saturdays and Holidays $3.50
Plus 20% U. S. Cabaret Tax
Minimum Check after 10:00 P. M. $2.50 per person of which Fifty Cents is a Cover charge, Plus 20% U. S. Cabaret Tax
Saturdays & Holidays $3.00 of which One Dollar is a Cover Charge,
Plus 20% U. S. Cabaret Tax
No Cover Charge for Dinner Guests Remaining after 10:00 P. M.
No Tables held after 8:00 P. M. for Dinner Show

---

### ★PALMERETTE

Seventy-three Cents

### DESSERTS

| | |
|---|---|
| *Palmer House Apple Pie . .30 | Home-made Cheese Cake . .30 |
| Rum Pie . . . . . . . . . .30 | Fig Custard Pudding, |
| Banana Jell-o Delight . . . .30 | Port Wine Sauce . . . . .30 |
| *Frozen Ice Cream Slice . . . .45 | Tutti Frutti Ice Cream . . .35 |
| *Palmer House Chocolate Ice Cream . . . . . . . . . . . . .35 | |

### CHEESE

| | |
|---|---|
| Cottage or Cream . . . . . .35 | Bel-Paese . . . . . . . . .45 |
| Camembert or Liederkranz . .35 | American Gorgonzola . . .35 |
| *Palmer House Cheese . . . .35 | |

### FRUIT

| | |
|---|---|
| Baked Apple 35; with Cream . . . . . . . . . . . . . . .40 |
| Delicious Apple . . . . . . .25 | Grapefruit . . . . . . . .35 |

### MILK, COFFEE, TEA, ETC.

| | |
|---|---|
| Tea . . . . . . . . . . .30 | Demi Tasse . . . . . . . .20 |
| Sanka Coffee or Kaffee Hag .40 | Chocolate or Cocoa . . . .35 |
| Postum . . . . . . . . . .35 | Certified Milk . . . . . .25 |
| Coffee, Pot . . . . . . . . . . . . . . . . . .30 | |

*Palmer House Rolls or Bread and Butter 15

(Bread, Rolls and Wheat Products Prepared in the Palmer House Bakery and Pastry Shop are Enriched with Vitamin "B")

Saccharine may be obtained from your Waiter on Request

Friday, February 8, 1946

★ ★ ★ ★ All prices are our ceiling prices, or below. By OPA regulation, our ceilings are based on our highest prices from April 4 to 10, 1943. Our menus or price lists for that week are available for your inspection. ★ ★ ★ ★

Pictured here is an extremely interesting dinner menu from the glory days of the Empire Room in 1946, shortly after the Second World War. Note that in a continuation of wartime rationing of fats, it is explicitly stated that only one piece of butter per person was provided! Prices were also still fixed, based on a "ceiling" of wartime highs dating to April 1943, and a stiff cabaret tax of 20 percent was in place as a means of raising war time revenues.

By the early 1970s, it became obvious that the nature of popular entertainment was changing and that the Empire Room could not compete with newer and larger entertainment venues. Phyllis Diller appeared as the last performer in the Empire Room during its tenure as a supper club. She is seen in this photograph with the late Ben Arden. On January 19, 1976, after 43 years, the world famous room went dark.

From its onset, The Palmer House touted its location as being the best in the city. This brochure from the 1940s shows the hotel amidst the financial and shopping districts of the city. Today, the hotel boasts being the closest major hotel to Millennium Park as well as to the Art Institute. In addition to being the best-located hotel in the city, The Palmer House also makes the claim, owing to its longevity, that it is the "Chicago hotel the world knows best."

By the early 1950s, the Conrad Hilton and The Palmer House were being marketed together as part of the expanding Hilton chain, which was at the time, headquartered at the Conrad Hilton hotel. Conrad Hilton had purchased both hotels in 1945. The similarity in their design, which is evident in the advertisement above, is attributable to the fact that both of the properties were built by the venerable Chicago architectural firm of Holabird and Roche in the mid 1920s.

Pres. Harry Truman is escorted into The Palmer House by long time General Manager Vernon Herndon in June of 1948. The Palmer House was the first stop on a presidential visit to the western United States. On this occasion, the president was feted at a banquet in the hotel's Crystal Room. Since the opening of the second Palmer House, the hotel has played host to every United States president from Ulysses S. Grant to William J. Clinton.

Another popular venue in The Palmer House that has existed for nearly half a century is Trader Vics, which opened on the lower level of the hotel in 1957 as "The Traders" and subsequently took the name "Trader Vics" in honor of the restaurant's founder, "Trader Vic" Bergeron. When the South Seas Island-themed restaurant opened, the *Chicago Sun Times* columnist Irv Kupcinet opined in his column that "the Traders in The Palmer House is the talk of our town's gourmet set." Forty five years later, a 2002 *Chicago Tribune* dining article referred to Trader Vics as "the grand daddy of the Tiki-bar genre."

By the late 1950s, The Palmer House was accommodating 6 million phone calls a year. A staff of 17 operators was kept busy placing the calls, which during peak periods came in at a rate of 2,700 per hour.

In 1959, The Palmer House switched to a direct-dial phone system, which allowed guests to place calls without having to use the operators. This necessitated the installation of miles of new cables as this photograph from the period attests.

*THE MOST UNIQUE IDEA IN*
*THE HISTORY OF HOTEL-KEEPING...*

 TWO COMPLETE FLOORS DEVOTED TO THOSE WHO SEEK
THE ULTIMATE IN EXCLUSIVENESS, PRIVACY AND ELEGANCE

## Palmer House Towers

The top two floors (twenty-second and twenty-third) of the Palmer House have been created for those who seek the very finest hotel accommodations. Here, in a world all its own, are two hundred and seventy rooms and suites with services, luxuries and an atmosphere unequaled in Chicago, or perhaps the entire world. Palmer House Towers is especially dedicated to a discerning clientele, who will recognize immediately that high above the heart of Chicago is an exclusive haven for guests who can be satisfied with nothing less than the finest.

In the early 1960s, The Palmer House became the first hotel in the country to pioneer "the towers" concept, which is now also commonly referred to in the hospitality industry as a concierge level or executive level. The top two floors of the hotel became a "hotel within a hotel" complete with a private reception area, a private barbershop, and a lounge that included the then novel concept of an honor bar. The advertisement above makes the claim that "the towers" is actually "the most unique idea in the history of hotel keeping."

This publicity photograph from the onset of The Palmer House Towers in the early 1960s shows white-gloved receptionists and tuxedoed concierges at the disposal of guests. Publicity from the period describes The Towers as "secluded" and "luxurious" and claims that you can arrive and depart the hotel "without ever seeing the lobby." One advertisement for The Towers concluded by making the following recommendation: "Send your out-of-town guests to The Palmer House Towers—the distinguished hotel that crowns Chicago's distinguished hotel."

Entertainment changed radically at The Palmer House between the 1950s and the 1960s as evidenced by the photographs juxtaposed on this page. In 1952, the staid Oak Room bar and lounge opened in the hotel with the attraction of a "30-inch TV for the viewing of special events." The bar was reserved for men only until 6:00 p.m.

As the go-go dancers in this photograph attest to, in the 1960s, one of the most swinging venues in The Palmer House was the lounge of the Town and Country restaurant, located on the hotel's lower level.

The Palmer House guest room décor also changed markedly between the 1950s and 1960s. In the 1950s, traditional décor was still in vogue as evidenced by this bedroom.

However, by the early 1960s a more modern motif was adopted as illustrated by the furnishings in this Palmer House suite. Note even the art work was adopted to satisfy more modern sensibilities.

These two views show The Palmer House lobby as it appeared in the period between the 1950s and the 1970s. So renowned is this venerable space that *The Encyclopedia of Chicago* makes mention of it by stating, "The Palmer House's palatial lobby, conceived as a European drawing room remains one of the most magnificent in the world."

In late 1962, Conrad Hilton personally announced a $10 million renovation plan for The Palmer House, which included the creation of an indoor pool and enclosed patio to be constructed in one of the interior courts of the hotel. Here, Conrad Hilton (left) examines a rendering of the project along with Palmer House General Manager Vernon Herndon.

The pool and patio when constructed bore only a superficial resemblance to the rendering. Though Chicago newspaper accounts of the period announced that a "huge indoor pool" was planned as part of the renovation project, structural and space impediments kept the pool, seen at the far end of this photograph, from living up to its press billing.

Another result of the $10 million renovation plan announced in 1962 was Palmer's Pub, which opened on the State Street side of the hotel in 1964. The two-story pub featured a deep red and mahogany Victorian décor, which created an atmosphere reminiscent of the fabled second Palmer House. Today the space is occupied by the Beef and Brandy restaurant.

In the early 1960s, The Palmer House opened one of the first kosher kitchens in any downtown Chicago hotel, which enabled it to capture a substantial portion of the Jewish event market. An advertisement for the kitchen dating to its opening makes note that the facility was under "the strict supervision of the Chicago Rabbinical Council."

This photograph of an "all staff" meeting at The Palmer House dating from the mid 1960s illustrates the rich diversity in both the attire and composition of the hotel's employees. A cosmopolitan air has always emanated from Chicago's grand hotels, and as such, they have long been willing employers of recent immigrants to the city from around the world. That tradition continues in The Palmer House today where over 30 different languages are spoken by employees.

Palmer House General Manager Vernon Herndon stands amidst a group of his employees being honored in January of 1962. Note the blackboards behind them, which keep track of the hotel's actual room occupancy and food and beverage covers on a monthly basis. Modernized versions of such boards are still in use by hotels today to keep employees apprised of the hotel's success rate.

Prince Charles of the United Kingdom (second from left) arrives at the arcade level of The Palmer House Hilton on October 19, 1977 for a civic dinner hosted by Mayor and Mrs. Michael Bilandic on behalf of the citizens of Chicago.

The dinner hosted in honor of Prince Charles at The Palmer House was held in the Grand Ballroom. At the event Mayor Michael Bilandic presented Prince Charles with honorary Chicago citizenship.

Former Chicago mayor, Harold Washington (second from left) shares a laugh with chefs from the Irish culinary team during St. Patrick's Day activities at The Palmer House in 1985. The charismatic Washington was a frequent guest of The Palmer House during his tenure as Mayor often serving as the opening speaker for various conventions held at the hotel.

Chicago's current Mayor Richard M. Daley is also a frequent guest of The Palmer House, and by tradition each year, The Palmer House bakes the mayor's official birthday cake. Here, Daley is pictured on his birthday with former Palmer House Executive Chef Daniel LaGarde.

The famous ceiling of The Palmer House lobby is roughly the size of a basketball court and is composed of 21 individual paintings that were produced in France by muralist Louis Pierre Rigal and shipped to the hotel in 1926. Each painting, such as the one above, depicts a scene from classical Greek mythology.

Noted Italian art restorer Lido Lippi pictured above was commissioned to restore the ceiling of The Palmer House to its previous glory in advance of The Palmer House's 125th anniversary ceremony in 1996. Lippi, who actually worked on the restoration of the Sistine Chapel, was dubbed The "Michelangelo of The Palmer House" in a *Chicago Sun Times* article on the ceiling's restoration. He spent over eight months painstakingly restoring the ceiling in a tedious inch by inch process.

This is the lobby of The Palmer House as it appears today. No less a journalistic authority than George F. Will dedicated an entire syndicated newspaper column to the joys of The Palmer House Lobby referring to it as the "essence of lobbiness" and concluding that, "All in all, The Palmer House lobby is like the Sistine Chapel without the chapel's infernal roar of tourists cameras clicking."

In 1996, The Palmer House commemorated its 125th anniversary with a grand celebration in front of the hotel's Monroe Street entrance. On the occasion Mayor Richard M. Daley, pictured at the podium, stated, "The Palmer House and Chicago share a long and proud history. The Empire Room, for example, is legendary, not just for the great performers who once played there, but for the equally famous people in the audience. It continues to be one of Chicago's favorites." Seen applauding Daley in the white coat is entertainer Carol Channing, who was present for the 125th anniversary of the hotel as she was present for the 100th anniversary. Seated to the right of Channing is actress Eartha Kitt, who also came for the occasion.

As part of the 125th anniversary celebration, The Palmer House Hilton General Manager Ted Ratcliff, standing next to podium, unveiled a street sign designating the block of Monroe Street adjacent to the hotel as "Palmer House Hilton Way."

Another feature of The Palmer House Hilton's 125th anniversary celebration was the reuniting of the Abbott Dancers, who had appeared for decades at the Empire Room. Many of them went on to marry very well amongst the legions of "stage door Johnnies," who sought their affection. Here, the dancers surround the legendary Palmer House Hilton Public Relations Director Ken Price, who has served the hotel in this capacity for nearly a quarter century. Price, known for his unique trademark glasses and quick wit, is considered one of the foremost living authorities on the history of The Palmer House.

The world-renowned Danish pianist and entertainer Victor Borge met his wife while performing at the Empire Room of The Palmer House. In a touching tribute to her as she lay gravely ill, he returned to the hotel in July of 2000 to take photographs of the legendary room where they met. On this occasion, he took time to perform an impromptu concert for Danish–American employees of The Palmer House, hotel manager Chris Hansen, left, and Jens Almborg.

This is the Empire Room as it looks today. The venue has been referred to as "the most beautiful public space in Chicago." Today it is used for VIP catering functions, and the facility still evokes a great nostalgia. Speaking to the *Chicago Tribune* in 1995, the famous Chicago civic leader and bon vivant Judge Abraham Lincoln Marovitz said of the Empire Room, "Neighborhoods change. Dress codes change. But when you walk in the Empire Room today, it does something to you. It brings back the world the way it once was."

Another function space of The Palmer House with a rich history is the Red Lacquer Ballroom, which dates back to the inception of the third Palmer House. Reminiscent of a ballroom of a king's palace, the Red Lacquer Room features richly enameled red walls and lustrous chandeliers with garnet drops. The *Chicago Tribune* selected the space as one of Chicago's "architectural jewels."

Like both The Drake and The Hilton Chicago, The Palmer House has been the set for several movies because of its unique and well-known features. In the photograph above, actor turned California Governor Arnold Schwarzenegger strides across The Palmer House lobby in a scene from the 1998 comedy thriller *Red Heat*. The Palmer House was also used as a set in the movies *Curly Sue* and in the horror film *The Relic*, which was filmed in the hotel's cavernous sub basements.

Pres. Bill Clinton has had a long association with The Palmer House. In the Oval Office he kept two photographs taken in the hotel. One photograph was of his parents in the Empire Room. The second was a photograph of he and Hillary Clinton taken in the midst of his successful bid to win the Illinois Democratic primary election. During the primary campaign, Clinton resided at The Palmer House. As such, he always held the hotel in high esteem and when he desired a venue in Chicago to say "thank you" to his Illinois supporters at the end of his presidency he chose The Palmer House lobby. In this photograph from the occasion, Clinton addresses his supporters, which include Mayor Richard M. Daley and former U.S. Commerce Secretary Bill Daley who can be seen at the base of the staircase.

# THREE

# THE DRAKE 1920–1960

Commenting on the extremely favorable and valuable location of The Drake, the late actor Peter Ustinov once said, "Each step you take in The Drake Hotel is like walking on diamonds." But it wasn't always that way. When an enterprising and insightful young architect by the name of Ben Marshall persuaded brothers John and Tracy Drake to build their new namesake hotel at the intersection of Lake Shore Drive and "Upper" Michigan Avenue, the area was only a remote corner of the city's "downtown." But its location opposite Oak Street Beach gave the hotel an immediate opportunity to be billed as one of the nation's first urban resorts.

The Drake brothers were second-generation hoteliers. Their father John Burroughs Drake had operated Chicago's Grand Pacific Hotel, which was a rival of the second Palmer House, and the family also ran the city's historic Blackstone on South Michigan Avenue. Like Potter Palmer before them and like Ernest Stevens after them, the Drake brothers set out to build upon their hotel knowledge in order to create a new structure that would inspire awe and emulation.

When Ben Marshall advanced the plans for The Drake in March of 1919, *The Economist*, a real-estate trade journal of the period, reported that the structure would be "of unusual magnificence, nothing like it in appearance, arrangement or finishing having ever been attempted in this country." Marshall was so enthused about the project that he waved his architectural fees in exchange for an ownership share in the hotel. He remained involved in many aspects of the hotel subsequent to its construction, including interior designs, entertainment, and even the designs of employee uniforms.

The hotel cost $10 million to build, including land, building, and furnishings. Nine hundred employees served its original 800 guest rooms. The Drake opened officially on New Year's Eve 1920 with a gala dinner for 2,000 of Chicago's leading citizens.

Throughout the 1920s, the fame of The Drake spread first across the country and subsequently across the world. WGN's first radio studio was perched on the top of The Drake, and it was from here where the famous "Amos and Andy" radio show originated and was broadcast live along with the big bands that performed at the hotel. In 1924, HRH the Prince of Wales (later known as the Duke of Windsor) was a guest of The Drake thus establishing The Drake's 81-year tradition of serving as the Chicago home to Britain's royal family. While the British royals have attended events at other larger hotels in the city, The Drake has always been their official headquarters in Chicago. Future British Prime Minister Winston S. Churchill was also a guest of The Drake during the 1920s, as were such notables as exiled Grand Duke Alexander of Russia and Queen Marie of Romania.

The 1930s saw the parade of famous guests continue at The Drake, but the onset of the decade, which coincided with the depths of the Great Depression, brought about a change in ownership at the hotel as the property was purchased by the Brashears family of Chicago, which formed a partnership with the ever present Ben Marshall known as the National Realty and Investment Company. In 1937, Edwin L. Brashears Sr., then president of The Drake, leased the hotel to the Kirkeby brothers' hotel group, which ran the hotel for nearly a decade until Edwin L. Brashears Sr. returned from military service in World War II in 1946.

In the late 1940s, the Brashears family set out to re-establish The Drake as the premiere luxury hotel in Chicago. By 1950, it was the first hotel in Chicago to have all of its guest rooms air conditioned. It would later be the first to have color televisions in all its guest rooms.

But some seeming anachronisms remained at The Drake simply because it was felt that they resulted in better guest service. For example, The Drake was the last Chicago hotel to go to direct dial telephone because it was believed that the operator could do more for the guest, and at the onset of the 1970s, The Drake was the only hotel in Chicago that still retained elevator operators. In addition, The Drake made its own ice cubes until 1967, refusing to go to ice machines until the quality of product that the ice machines produced was deemed comparable to the "hand made cubes."

This alluring combination of new amenities and traditional, exacting service standards kept The Drake on top of the Chicago hotel market throughout the 1950s and 1960s and well into the 1970s. As the *Chicago Tribune* put it in a February 2005 article on The Drake, "From its birth in 1920 until its sheen was eclipsed by the debut of the Ritz-Carlton Chicago in 1974, The Drake was *the* Chicago oasis for visiting kings, queens, diplomats and entertainers."

John Burroughs Drake was one of America's most noteworthy hoteliers. A native of Lebanon, Ohio, he was born in 1826 and arrived in Chicago while not yet 30. He eventually became proprietor of the Tremont Hotel, which burnt in the Great Chicago Fire of 1871. Not one to wallow in his misfortune, while the fire was still burning he negotiated for the Michigan Avenue Hotel at Congress and Michigan. The panicked owner was only too happy to sell the hotel to Drake, who had the last laugh after correctly predicting that the fire would bypass the hotel. From this hotel, which he re-christened the Tremont House, he went on to take control of the venerable Grand Pacific Hotel where he presided for 20 years and gained an international reputation as a bon vivant, connoisseur, and popular host. Drake died in 1895, but his sons followed in his footsteps establishing themselves as hoteliers and naming The Drake Hotel in their father's honor.

Benjamin Marshall, the flamboyant self taught architect of The Drake and many other notable Chicago structures, including the Blackstone Hotel, the Blackstone Theater, and the Edgewater Beach Hotel, Marshall was instrumental in all aspects of The Drake for 20 years. He initially served as vice president of The Drake's parent company, the Whitestone Company, and subsequently even served as the hotel's general manager and director of entertainment. An intimate friend of the legendary show business impresario Flo Ziegfield, Marshal had an appreciation of drama and theatrics that he put to excellent use in the events that he orchestrated at The Drake.

The oldest son of John Burroughs Drake, Tracy C. Drake was responsible for the development of both the Blackstone and The Drake Hotels. After attending schools on the East Coast and traveling through Europe, Tracy Drake returned to Chicago to begin learning all aspects of the hotel business from the bottom up at his father's Grand Pacific Hotel. He proved to be a quick study. In the book *Chicago and its Makers*, it is noted that while apprenticing in the hotel's culinary department, Drake became so proficient in carving that "he could carve a 13-pound turkey in the record time of 5 minutes serving 23 orders and leaving nothing but bones"—an accomplishment that few hotel men can boast of today. Later he turned his considerable skills to "carving" business deals. He built the Blackstone in 1910 and The Drake a decade later. He served as the president of the Whitestone Company, the parent company of The Drake.

The namesake of his father, John B. Drake was the second born Drake brother. Like his older brother, he completed his education on the East Coast, was dispatched on an around the world trip, and returned to begin working at his father's Grand Pacific Hotel. Subsequently, he went to work with Illinois Trust and Savings, acquiring a financial knowledge that would serve him and his brother well in their business dealings to construct and operate the Blackstone and The Drake. John B. Drake served as treasurer of the Whitestone Company, the parent company of The Drake. It is for John and Tracy Drake that the Drake Brothers Steak House in The Drake hotel is named. There was also a third Drake brother named Francis who, while not an officer in The Drake Hotel's parent company, did serve as a director in his brothers' hotel enterprises.

This is a classic photograph of bathers on Oak Street Beach opposite The Drake dating from the early 1920s. The original 1920 brochure of The Drake emphasized its proximity to Lake Michigan by stating that the hotel "combines all the pleasures of the most attractive summer resort with the comfort of a luxurious metropolitan hotel and the advantages of a great city."

## Chicago's Wonderful Hotel

FAR-FAMED is THE DRAKE and its favored location on the restful shores of Lake Michigan, adjoining Lincoln Park. And yet the center of the city's business and theatrical districts is close at hand.

Whether you come to Chicago as a business visitor or as a vacationist, THE DRAKE offers unrivaled advantages. Come and find perfect summer-time enjoyment. Bathing, tennis, horse-back riding, Atlantic City chairs and other pleasures await you all season long. Play for THE DRAKE cup on the Lincoln Park Golf Course.

Suites and rooms with bath to suit every reasonable requirement. Attractive discounts for extended periods. *Write for booklet.*

# The DRAKE

## Lake Shore Drive and Upper Michigan Avenue, CHICAGO

Under direction of The Drake Hotel Co., owners of **THE BLACKSTONE** (on South Michigan Ave., only a short distance away)

This aerial photograph dating from the mid-1920s illustrates just how little development existed in the neighborhood surrounding The Drake shortly after the hotel opened. Note the number of vacant land parcels east of Michigan Avenue in what is now Streeterville.

This early advertisement for The Drake is interesting in that it promotes "horse-back riding" as one of the amenities available for guests of the hotel. The advertisement also emphasizes the joint ownership between The Drake and the older, more established Blackstone Hotel on South Michigan Avenue.

The Drake's architect, Ben Marshall, took his inspiration for the design of the hotel from the Italian palaces of High Renaissance Rome and Florence. Constructed of smooth limestone, the building is 14 stories high. It rises from a rectangular base, which changes at the third story to an H-shape. A distinctive feature of Italian Renaissance design found in The Drake is the "Piano Nobile," or principle story raised above ground and containing the public rooms. The base level of the hotel featured an arcade containing a number of services, such as barber shops and changing rooms so that guests could freshen up from their journey to the hotel and look presentable before making their "grand entrance" on to the Piano Nobile.

This opening advertisement of The Drake illustrates that the hotel positioned itself to be a luxury hotel from its inception. Consider that, according to the advertisement, single rooms with a bath started at $5 per night and upward. Meanwhile, The Stevens, which opened seven years after The Drake, began with rates of only $3.50 per night and upward for a single room including a bath. With the views of Lake Michigan afforded to guests of The Drake, one might think that the most expensive rooms would have been on the top floors. However, the top two floors of the hotel were originally reserved for the butlers, chauffeurs, and personal attendants of the guests who traveled to the hotel. The reason being that heat rises, and there was not air conditioning yet.

*The Literary Digest for April 16, 1921*    53

## Chicago's Wonderful New Hotel

*A*S a guest of this ideally-located, beautiful new hotel you will be in a position to appreciate the real charm of America's second city.

THE DRAKE is on the quiet shore of Lake Michigan, five minutes from the heart of the city. As a guest you are near the center of things, yet you *live* in the quiet of a favored residential section overlooking the Lake and Lincoln Park.

The memory of a sojourn at THE DRAKE will surely intensify the pleasure of a visit to Chicago, hailed more and more as one of the queen summer-pleasure cities of the world.

*Single Rooms, each with bath, $5 per day and upward*
*Rooms for two, as low as $3 for each person*

*Booklet sent, on request*

## The DRAKE

Lake Shore Drive and Upper Michigan Avenue
CHICAGO

THE DRAKE is under the direction of the Drake Hotel Company, owners of THE BLACKSTONE
*(Six minutes distant by taxicab)*

309.                    THE DRAKE, CHICAGO'S WONDERFUL NEW HOTEL.

An early post card of The Drake clearly shows the park that existed directly to the east of the hotel when it was first opened. The Drake maintained a popular screened terrace facing this park where guests could enjoy cold drinks and dancing during the warm summer months. Subsequent to the building of The Drake Tower adjacent to the hotel, the terrace was enclosed and is now the Walton Room. Note also that the postcard shows three skylights that were located just above the Gold Coast Room on the north side of the hotel. These skylights, which were retractable, served to ventilate the Gold Coast Room.

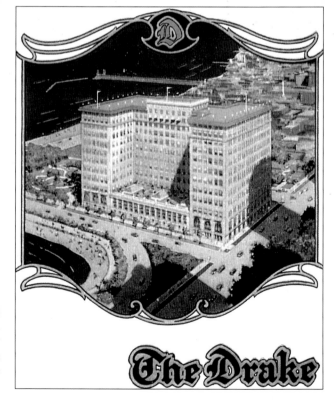

Seen here is a Drake luggage tag from shortly after the hotel's opening. Nearly all major hotels the 1920s and 1930s provided these stickers to their guests, many of whom collected them as souvenirs and placed them on their suitcases to denote the many places they had visited. The park seen in front of the hotel on Walton Street in this stylized rendering was soon cleared to make a parking facility for The Drake and the surrounding businesses.

ANNUAL BANQUET
AMERICAN SOCIETY FOR STEEL TREATING
DRAKE HOTEL SEPT. 23, 1926

KAUFMANN & FABRY CO.
CHICAGO
26-6863

Soon after its inauguration, The Drake established a reputation as the venue of choice for the most prestigious upper-class events and banquets in the city. This photograph was taken in the Grand Ballroom of The Drake on September 23, 1922. It is typical of the staged photographs that were taken at events in the ballrooms of all grand hotels throughout the 1920s through the 1940s. Most of these types of photographs were made into two-foot-long prints and were presented as a souvenir of the occasion.

The Fountain Court (also known as the Reception Court and subsequently the Palm Court) was always a center of activity at The Drake. At various points throughout the 1920s, there were ducks and even baby alligators swimming in the fountain pond seen in the center of this photograph. The appeal of the Reception Court and other public spaces of The Drake was such that in 1921, *Good Furniture* magazine extolled the hotel for creating "a reposeful spirit of welcome and home surroundings planned in a large and, to be sure, more or less monumental way. It stands to the credit of the architects that the ideal of the hotel has found such appealing and noble expression."

Initially, the Gold Coast Room, which is now used for important banquets, was the main dining room of The Drake and home to many big band performances. During this period, each summer the Gold Coast Room was transformed into the Silver Forest Room. When the warm weather arrived, the heavy carpets of winter were lifted, and the columns were painted with silver vines, and the room took on the cool colors of blue and white. The skylights in the ceiling were then opened to allow the cool lake breezes to refresh this room. In the winter, the room was repainted gold and cream.

BANQUET in honor of Her Royal Highness Crown Princess Martha of Norway Drake Hotel May 4, 1939

By the late 1930s, the Gold Coast Room had become the prestigious banqueting facility as we know it today. In this photograph, ladies are gathered for a banquet in honor of Her Royal Highness Crown Princess Martha of Norway. The crown princess was but one of the many notable figures to have visited The Drake in the 1930s. Between 1932 and 1936 alone, celebrities such as Pres. Herbert Hoover, Cecil B. DeMille, Bing Crosby, George Gershwin, Walt Disney, Kathryn Hepburn, Gugliemo Marconi, Amelia Earhart, Walter Winchell, Gloria Swanson, Sinclair Lewis, and Charles Lindbergh visited the hotel.

The Drake Hotel's legendary Cape Cod Room opened in 1933 for Chicago's Century of Progress Exhibition World's Fair. An early brochure highlighting the hotel's dining options describes the restaurant as follows: "When you step into the Cape Cod Room . . . you enter the tangy atmosphere of the New England Coast. Here you find Chicago's finest and most unusual sea food restaurant." The room has changed little in the past 70 years. It is still adorned with nautical paraphernalia as well as with exposed wood beams, hanging copper pots, and stuffed sailfish.

Another Chicago institution found at The Drake is the Coq d'Or bar located on the arcade level of the hotel. The Coq d'Or acquired a memorable role in the history of the city when it became the second bar in Chicago to serve drinks to guests on December 6, 1933, the date which marked the end of 14 years of Prohibition in the state of Illinois. On that memorable evening, guests had arrived long before the 8:30 p.m. call announcing the repeal. The lines were so long that the bartenders only had time to pour whiskey at 40¢ a glass. The celebration lasted until dawn.

By the mid 1940s, the skyline surrounding The Drake had change markedly. The Drake Towers apartment building was built adjacent to the hotel, and the Palmolive building rose from behind it on Walton Street. It was at this time that The Drake's landmark sign was installed on the roof of the hotel.

By January 1941, the Gold Coast Room was once again redecorated, this time in turquoise and coral with gold leaf tracery on the stately pillars. In 1982, the room was restored to the original colors of gold and cream, at a cost of $1.3 million, with new chandeliers of French crystal, new air conditioning, sound system and lighting, carpet, draperies, and thermopane windows.

In the 1940s, the Fountain Court underwent a major renovation. The fountain was deepened, an urn centered in it, and the overall décor was lightened. In the summer, the room took on a gardenlike setting. In the winter, however, a 2,000-pound fire place hood was suspended from the ceiling, and the marble base of the fountain was transformed into a fire place that set the winter, holiday tone.

The copy for an early ad for the Camellia House read, "Dine in the charming Camellia House . . . where discriminating people gather. Enjoy extraordinary cuisine served to your individual taste. And for your added pleasure, there is music during luncheon and dancing every evening." One of The Drake's own brochures described the Camellia House as "truly one of the most enchanting night spots ever created. Here one may enjoy a unique and refreshing atmosphere, excellent dance music and food that set a new standard for Chicago's gourmets."

For over 30 years in the golden era of supper clubs, The Drake's Camellia House reigned as one of the most popular venues of its type in the city. Dorothy Draper was hired to design the Camellia House, and it was completed in January 1941. Both the china and the carpeting had big pink camellias in their design.

## A La Carte

**HORS-d'OEUVRES**

| | | | |
|---|---|---|---|
| Little Neck Clams 60 | Bluepoints 55 | Cotuits 60 | Cherrystone Clams 65 |
| Seafood Supreme 85 | Fresh Shrimp Cocktail 75 | | Canape Anchovy 75 |
| Fresh Crabmeat Cocktail 80 | Orange Juice 35 | | Grapefruit Juice 35 |
| Chilled Tomato Juice Cocktail 30 | | Imported Beluga Caviar 2.75 | |
| Assorted Hors-d'Oeuvres 90 | Canape Domestic Caviar 1.25 | Domestic Caviar 1.75 | |
| Bismark Herring 65 | Antipasto 75 | Fresh Fruit Supreme 75 | |
| Tomato, Ravigotte 65 | | French Sardines, Boneless or Peeled 90 | |
| Filet of Imported Wine Herring 65 | | Fresh Lobster Supreme 1.25 | |
| | Imported Beluga Caviar Canape 2.25 | | |

**SOUPS**

| | | | |
|---|---|---|---|
| Chicken Gumbo 50 | Chicken Broth 45; Tureen 60 | | Tomato Bouillon 35 |
| Consomme, Bellevue 50 | Clear Green Turtle 60 | | Clam Broth 40 |
| Plain Consomme 40 | Onion Soup au Gratin 60 (to order) | | Cream of Tomato 45 |
| Oyster or Clam Stew 60; half and half 75; Cream Stew 90 | | | Puree of Peas 45 |

**RELISHES**

| | | |
|---|---|---|
| Sweet or Dill Pickles 25 | | Pickled Walnuts 35 |
| Radishes 25 | Spanish Queen or Ripe California Olives 45 | |
| Stuffed Celery 55 | Chow Chow 30 | Celery Hearts 35 |

**FRESH FISH TO ORDER**

| | | |
|---|---|---|
| Lake Superior Whitefish 1.10 | Salt Mackerel 80 | Frog Legs 1.00 |
| Broiled Half Lobster 1.75 | Soft Shell Crabs 1.25 | Halibut Steak 90 |
| Broiled Salmon Steak 1.00 | Pompano 1.25 | Shad Roe with Bacon 1.25 |
| Broiled Sardines 70 | Imported English Sole 1.25 | Domestic Sole 1.00 |
| Fresh or Spanish Mackerel 80 | Filet of Pike, Saute, Meuniere 90 | |
| Lake Trout 1.00 | | Brook Trout 1.25 |

**POULTRY, STEAKS, CHOPS, Etc.**

| | | |
|---|---|---|
| Young Turkey, Sage Dressing 1.35 | | Prime Ribs of Beef 1.35 |
| Pork Chop 85 | Lamb Chops (2) 1.25 | Mutton Chop 1.25 |
| Broiled Chicken (half) 1.50 | | Broiled Spring Chicken 1.50 |
| Broiled Jumbo Squab 1.50 | | Guinea Hen (half), Broiled 1.50 |
| Filet Mignon 2.50 | | Boneless Stuffed Squab Chicken 1.50 |
| Pork Tenderloin 1.00 | | Small Steak 2.00 |
| Breaded Veal Cutlet, Tomato Sauce 1.00 | | Mixed Grill, Blackstone 1.50 |
| Steak, Minute 2.00 | | Mutton Chop Combination 1.50 |
| Broiled Fresh Pig's Feet 80 | Tenderloin or Sirloin Steak, for (1) 2.75:(2) 5.00 | |
| Broiled Sweetbreads 1.50 | | Calf's Liver 90 |
| Broiled Veal Kidney 80 | | Steak, Minute, Blackstone 2.50 |
| English Mutton Chop 1.25 | | Country Sausage Cakes 80 |

**FARINAGES AND SAVORIES**

| | | |
|---|---|---|
| Ravioli Italienne 65 | Noodles, Polonaise 55 | Macaroni au Gratin 55 |
| Spaghetti, Caruso 65 | Welsh Rarebit 75 | Kniokis au Gratin 60 | Golden Buck 90 |

**FRESH VEGETABLES**

| | | |
|---|---|---|
| New String Beans 45 | Beets in Butter 40 | Artichoke Hollandaise 60 |
| Carrots 40 | Broccoli Hollandaise 60 | Grilled or Fried Tomatoes 50 |
| New Lima Beans 50 | | Brussels Sprouts 50 |
| Fried Parsnips 40 | New Peas 45 | Fresh Spinach 45; in Cream 50 |
| Braised Celery 60 | Hubbard Squash 45 | Cauliflower, Hollandaise 50 |
| Fried Egg Plant 45 | Succotash 45 | Mashed White or Yellow Turnips 50 |

**CANNED VEGETABLES**

| | | | |
|---|---|---|---|
| Lima Beans 45 | Wax or String Beans 40 | French Peas 60 | Stewed Corn 45 |
| | White Asparagus, Hollandaise or Vinaigrette 65 | | |

**POTATOES**

| | | | | |
|---|---|---|---|---|
| Special Baked 35 | French Fried 35 | Grilled 35 | Souffle 45 | Au Gratin 45 |
| Saute 35 | Mashed 25 | New Broiled 30 | Cream 40 | Idaho Baked 30 |
| Sweet Potatoes 30 | Baked 30 | Candied 40 | Grilled 35 | Fried 35 |

**SALADS**

| | | | |
|---|---|---|---|
| Salad Evelyn 55 | Hearts of Palm 1.00 | Blackstone 60 | Lobster 1.75 | Lettuce 40 |
| Combination 60 | Chicory 40 | Fresh Fruit 75 | Cucumber 45 | Romaine 45 |
| Alligator Pear, Half 50 | Artichoke, Vinaigrette 65 | | Vegetable 65 |
| Crabmeat 90 | Chicken (white meat) 1.50 | Shrimp 85 | Tomato 40 |
| Asparagus Tips 55 | Grape Fruit 55 | Potato Salad 40 | Cole Slaw 40 |

**COLD DISHES**

| | |
|---|---|
| Smoked Salmon, Marie Garden 90 | Smoked Sturgeon a la Russe 1.25 |
| Assorted Cold Meat 1.25; with Chicken 1.50 | Roast Rib of Beef 1.40 |
| | Half Lobster, Mayonnaise 1.85 |
| Westphalian Ham with Cold Slaw 1.10 | Sliced Chicken 1.50 |
| Virginia Ham 1.00 | Ham 90 | Rack of Pork, Potato Salad 90 |
| Smoked Beef Tongue 90 | Whitefish in Jelly 1.00 |
| Boned Pigs' Feet in Jelly, Salad Printaniere 80 | Salmon in Jelly 95 |

**SANDWICHES**

| | | | |
|---|---|---|---|
| Tongue 50 | Domestic Caviar 1.00 | Sardine 75 | Ham 50 |
| Steak 1.50 | Egg and Anchovy 80 | Chicken 90 | Chicken Salad 90 |
| Imported Swiss Cheese 50 | Cold Roast Beef 90; Hot 1.10 | | Club 1.00 |

**PASTRY AND PIES**

| | | |
|---|---|---|
| Napoleon Cream Slice 25 | | Assorted Cake 25 |
| Macaroons 25 | Meringue Chantilly 30 | Chocolate Eclair 25 |
| Pound Cake 25 | Fruit Cake 35 | Assorted French Pastry 25 |
| Crepes Suzette 1.25 | Apple Pie 25 | Petit Fours 25 | Cocoanut Custard Pie 25 |
| Fresh Peach Shortcake 50 | Charlotte Russe 35 | Lady Fingers 25 |

**ICE CREAMS, ICES**

| | | | |
|---|---|---|---|
| Frozen Egg Nogg 45 | Biscuit Tortoni 35 | Charlotte Glace 40 | Peach Melba 75 |
| French Vanilla, Coffee, Pistachio, Chocolate Chip, | | | |
| | | Fresh Peach, Burnt Almond or Chocolate Ice Cream 35 | |
| Parfait Margurite 40 | | | Rainbow Parfait 40 |
| Lemon, Pineapple, Orange or Raspberry Ice 30 | | | Coupe Blackstone 45 |

**FRESH FRUITS**

| | | |
|---|---|---|
| Orange 25 | Tokay Grapes 35 | Grape Fruit, Half 35 |
| Apple 20 | Pear 20 | Compote of Fresh Fruits 50 | Sliced Fresh Pineapple 35 |

**CHEESE**

| | | | |
|---|---|---|---|
| Camembert 40 | Philadelphia Cream 35 | | Old English 40 |
| American 35 | Imported Swiss 40 | Gorgenzola 40 | Stilton 40 |
| Edam 30 | Imported Roquefort 40 | Cottage 35 | Brie 40 |
| Port du Salut 40 | Bel Paese 40 | Liederkranz 35 | Swiss Gruyere 40 |

**COFFEE, TEA, Etc.**

The Drake Special Blend Coffee with Cream, Pot for one 30
Fresh Churned Buttermilk
Guernse...
English Brea...
Butter, Sweet or Sa...

---

### CHEF'S SUGGESTIONS FOR DINNER

Consomme Madrilene .50      Cream of Asparagus, Chantilly .50
Fried Fresh Blue Point Oysters, Cole Slaw, Tartar Sauce, Julienne Potatoes .90
Stuffed Filets of English Sole au Plat, Normande 1.25
Filets of Wall Eyed Pike Saute, Nicoise 1.10
Medaillon of Jumbo Whitefish au Plat, Fecampoise 1.10
Broiled Fresh Delaware Shad Roe, Bacon, Mushrooms and
French Fried Potatoes 1.25
Grilled Live Baby Lobster, Paprika Butter, Cape Cod Style 2.00
Breast of Capon Saute, Drake, New Peas, Parisienne Potatoes 1.75
Roast Prime Ribs of Beef, Natural Gravy, Brussel Sprouts, Baked Potato 1.50
Smothered Royal Jumbo Squab, Southern Style, New Peas, Potato Croquette 1.50
Mignon of Beef Tenderloin Saute, Goose Liver, Perigueux Sauce,
Truffle, String Beans and Potato Croquette 2.75
Roast Turkey, Chestnut Dressing, New Peas, Candied Sweet Potatoes,
Cranberry Jelly 1.50
Braised Larded Calf's Sweetbreads, Jardiniere, Parisienne Potatoes 1.35

Evelyn Salad .65

Baba au Rum .40           Cherry Pie .25
Sunday, November 17th

---

This Drake's a-la-carte menu dates back to the 1940s. It is always interesting to note how culinary tastes have changed over the decades. Note that this menu offers such favorites of the period as "Boned Pigs Feet in Jelly," "Tongue Sandwiches," "Sardine Sandwiches," "Mutton Chops," "Welsh rarebit," "Clear Green Turtle Soup," "Beets in Butter," and a special of "Braised Larded Calf's Sweetbreads." Needless to say, these items are rarely found any longer on Drake menus.

The Cape Cod Room of The Drake is shown in this photograph, which dates back to the 1950s. It was in this period that the restaurant was frequented by celebrities such as Joe DiMaggio and Marilyn Monroe, who carved their initials into the Cape Cod Room's wooden bar top. People came from all over to try the restaurant's red snapper-based "bookbinder's soup," which is served with a small vile of sherry, which is then poured into the soup. The bookbinder's soup is still the most popular item served at The Drake today.

In the 1950s, the Coq d'Or underwent a transformation that included the installation of one of the first televisions to be placed in a Chicago bar. By this time, the bar was already a favorite haunt of Streeterville residents, as well as of reporters, politicians, and entertainers. It has changed little today. The leather backed chairs and warm wood paneling still evoke the feeling of a bygone "gentleman's drinking room."

Avenue One, a more contemporary dining venue. The large painting that hung on the wall of the Camellia House is visible in the photograph on the left and can now be found above the main entrance stairway of The Drake.

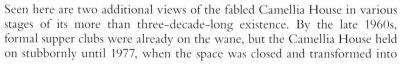

Seen here are two additional views of the fabled Camellia House in various stages of its more than three-decade-long existence. By the late 1960s, formal supper clubs were already on the wane, but the Camellia House held on stubbornly until 1977, when the space was closed and transformed into

In this classic 1968 photograph, 99 gentlemen are gathered at one long table in the Gold Coast Room of The Drake for a black tie dinner of the Les Amis d'Escoffier Society. The society venerates the famed French culinary master Auguste Escoffier. According to the traditions of the society, its members must all wear their napkins tucked into their shirts, and the 100th seat at the head of the table must be kept vacant in memory of Escoffier.

F O U R

# THE DRAKE 1960–2005

By the 1960s, The Drake was already long established as a Chicago icon. The hotel's Cape Cod Room was one of the city's most popular restaurants; its Coq d'Or was one of Chicago's best-loved bars; and its private Club International enjoyed a waiting list for membership. But the decade of the 1960s saw many longtime Chicagoans and regular patrons of The Drake begin to leave the city for the suburbs. Noting this trend, the Brashears family, which owned The Drake, decided to build another Drake hotel in the burgeoning western suburb of Oak Brook in 1962, which resulted in the now famous Drake Oak Brook.

The downtown Drake certainly afforded the financial opportunity for a sister hotel in the suburbs. According to an October 1970 article in *Hospitality* magazine, between the years of 1963 and 1966, while the average occupancy for Chicago hovered between 63 and 64 percent, "The Drake ran an even 80 percent."

In the 1970s, The Drake's occupancy was aided by the fact that North Michigan had overtaken State Street as the premiere shopping street in Chicago. The "obscure" location for the hotel selected by Ben Marshall was reaping handsome dividends half a century later when the city's downtown truly "caught up" to The Drake. As such, the hotel continued to attract a host of world leaders in the 1970s, including H.M. Emperor Hirohito of Japan in 1975 and H.R.H. Prince Charles of the Untied Kingdom in 1977. In 1979, the prestige of The Drake was still such that John Cardinal Cody, head of the Chicago Archdiocese and official host to Pope John Paul II when he visited Chicago that year, requested that the hotel cater the official dinners for Pope John Paul II, which were held at the cardinal's residence. The Drake obliged, and the Pope was served the hotel's famous bookbinder soup in addition to the club international salad, tail of whitefish, and California wines. Despite these notable successes, by the end of the 1970s, as the photographs in the ensuing chapter attest, many venues in The Drake were looking extremely dated and in need of considerable refurbishment.

In 1979, the Brashears partnership created a ground lease for The Drake whereby the family would continue to own the land on which the hotel sits but would lease The Drake building its self to a "tenant" who would own the physical hotel for the duration of the lease. The new owners of the hotel were financiers Jerold Wexler and Edward Ross.

On January 1, 1981, United Kingdom-based Hilton International, then operating in the United States as Vista Hotels, was brought in as the management company for The Drake. Hilton International pledged to the

City of Chicago to return the hotel to its previous splendor and embarked on a multi-year renovation that cost over $40 million to complete. In May of 1981, the 61-year-old Drake Hotel was accorded a high honor when it was placed on the National Register of Historic Places, joining other landmark structures in Chicago such as Louis Sullivan's Carson Pirie Scott building and the old Water Tower structure.

With Hilton International restoring The Drake to its traditional grandeur, the hotel became a set for several popular movies, including *The Blues Brothers*, *Risky Business*, *My Best Friends Wedding*, and *Hero* among others. According to the book *Hollywood on Lake Michigan*, filming of a key exterior scene at The Drake for the 1992 movie *Hero*, which starred Andy Garcia, Geena Davis, and Dustin Hoffman, had to be temporarily halted because at the same time Oprah Winfrey was hosting a tribute to Michael Jordan at the hotel and a "seemingly non-stop parade of limousines dropped off a coterie of high-powered luminaries," thereby preventing the filming as planned. Such is life at The Drake! *Hollywood on Lake Michigan* goes on to state, "Movie-wise, the Drake Hotel always rates high on the posh meter. In *Mission Impossible* (1996), a simple mention of 'a room at the Drake' is all it takes for secret agent Jon Voight to impress his colleagues in the international spy game—no mean shakes in a cinematic profession known for impeccably high standards."

In 1996, Hilton International acquired the lease interest on The Drake from a venture controlled by Edward Ross. Also in 1996, The Drake was front and center during one of the most high profile visits ever bestowed on Chicago when the late Princess Diana came to the city for three memorable days in June to help raise money for cancer research. Like generations of the British royal family before her, she made The Drake her residence in Chicago. JoAnn Bongiorno, then director of public relations for The Drake, recalled, "Our staff was enamored with her warmth, beauty, and accessibility. She did not shun anyone, but made them feel special. She'd walk in and anyone who had flowers she would walk over to and take the flowers and thank them."

In the last 10 years, The Drake has seen competition increase amongst North Michigan Avenue luxury hotels, but the venerable dowager of Chicago luxury hotels has one asset that most of its competitors lack. It is a true Chicago original with its roots right here in this city. Perhaps no other hotel in Chicago inspires more local loyalty than does The Drake where different generations of the same family routinely come to continue the traditions begun by their forefathers many decades ago.

Seen here is the legendary Sapphire Suite of The Drake, which was used for decades to accommodate visiting royalty and other notables. Amongst the past occupants of the suite were Queen Elizabeth II of the United Kingdom, Emperor Hirohito of Japan, King Carl Gustaf of Sweden, and Prince Charles and his aunt Princess Margaret of the United Kingdom.

These two views show Avenue One, the successor to the Camellia House. This cocktail lounge and dining venue was designed with the intention of keeping up with the changing times and adding some excitement to the hotel, but it was short lived. In 1982, the room closed and was transformed into a banqueting facility, which is today known as the Drake Room.

By the time Hilton International took over management of The Drake in December 1980, the Fountain Court, now renamed the Palm Court, was in desperate need of restoration and updating as you can see from the photographs on this page. Note the model of The Drake, which was on display in the Palm Court to commemorate the 60th anniversary of the hotel.

Another area of the hotel that needed renovation at the time Hilton International took over management of The Drake was the lobby. Plans for the renovation of the hotel under Hilton International's direction were immediately advanced and estimated at $6 million. However, before the initial restoration was complete, some $40 million had been spent to return the hotel to its previous grandeur.

The Palm Court is seen here subsequent to its renovation in the early 1980s. Chicago Mayor Jane Byrne was invited to turn on the renovated fountain in the center of the room for the first time, which she obligingly did at an event at the hotel dedicated to the United Cerebral Palsy Association. Today, the Palm Court of The Drake still reigns supreme as the most popular "tea room" in Chicago.

David Miller, a designer who had worked for Marshall Fields for over 30 years, was persuaded to come out of retirement to work on the 1981 restoration of The Drake. Amongst his legacies in the hotel is the 275-year-old French bronze urn that he found in the Florentine Craftsman House in New York and brought back to Chicago to use as the focal point of the renovated Palm Court.

From the 1960s to the early 1980s, the hotel's three-meal-a-day restaurant was the Raleigh Rooms, so named because the room was divided into three sections. Portraits of American generals hung on the wall and the room was decorated in patriotic red, white, and blue.

In 1983, when the Raleigh Rooms were being remodeled, it was noted while uncovering the walls that this venue had been known in a previous incarnation as the Oak Room, and as such, it was given the name of Oak Terrace. To complete the theme, it was provided with additional oak paneling as well as with brass, grass, and plenty of greenery. The room, which was popular for its beautiful views of the adjacent park and Lake Michigan, enjoyed a 20-year tenure before being converted to the new Drake Brothers Steak House in 2004.

This is the lobby of The Drake in 1998 when the space was updated with a dramatic look of midnight blue, red, and gold. The inset carpet was woven expressly for The Drake. The Drake lobby may well be an example of a classical space that looks more elegant now than it did when it first opened.

In 1996, a grant was provided to the City of Chicago to construct a park just north of The Drake to feature a gazebo surrounded by flowers. The park is dedicated to the victims of the Holocaust.

Benjamin Marshall, The Drake's architect, proved to be a visionary when he advocated that The Drake be located where Lake Shore Drive met Upper Michigan Avenue. Nearly 85 years after its inception, the spectacular views of Lake Michigan and the North Shore are still one of the principal selling features of The Drake. Many of the hotel's suites, such as the one pictured above, are designed to allow guests the maximum appreciation of the views.

Princess Diana arrives at The Drake where she stayed during her historic visit to Chicago in June 1996. She is accompanied by Martin Lawrence, who then served as general manager of The Drake. While staying at The Drake, she occupied the Presidential Suite, room No. 550.

# FIVE

# THE STEVENS

The world had never seen anything quite like The Stevens when its doors opened in May 1927. Its inauguration was considered such an important event that no less illustrious a figure than the vice president of the United States at the time, Charles G. Dawes, came to Chicago to have the honor of registering as the hotel's first guest.

What the vice president and others found when they came to The Stevens was a virtual city within a city with all the amenities necessary to make it completely self sufficient. The editor in chief of the *Hotel World* magazine said at the time that The Stevens was filled "with luxury and comfort beyond the dreams and imagination of the most imaginative."

The hotel reflected the immense vision of one man—Ernest J. Stevens. Stevens was a prominent Chicago hotelier who for several years had run the city's La Salle Hotel, which was constructed in 1909. Despite the considerable success of the La Salle, which already enjoyed a status as Chicago's largest hotel, Stevens soon began formulating the plans for another hotel that would be vastly different in scope.

When John Holabird of The Stevens's architectural firm of Holabird and Roche was asked what paramount idea was in the minds of the architects when they conceived the Hotel Stevens, he replied simply, "All of us merely tried to interpret Mr. E. J. Stevens's plans for a 'perfect' hotel—Quite incidentally, it is the world's largest. We just provided the architectural background for his ideas because he knew exactly what he wanted."

What he wanted was simply a hotel like no other that would offer the world's most extensive convention facilities for decades to come. The hotel was an immediate hit with the public, and the city of Chicago began using the hotel to fete famous visitors such as Charles Lindbergh, who was honored by the mayor of Chicago only three months after The Stevens had opened in August 1927. This tradition of hosting important visitors at The Stevens continues today, owing to one of the hotels most stunning achievements a magnificent Versailles-inspired Grand Ballroom that is completely free of visible structural pillars due to an elaborate and technologically advanced system of underground supporting pillars, caissons, and trusses.

Unfortunately, the ravages of the Great Stock Market Crash and the subsequent Depression that began in 1929 took their toll on The Stevens. By June 1934, the hotel was declared insolvent, and the equity of preferred and common shareholders was wiped out. Only the conversion of some of the rooms into apartments in 1935 as part of a reorganization plan kept the hotel afloat. But the damage had been done. By the end of the 1930s, The Stevens, which was built for $30 million, was appraised for only $7 million.

Like much of the rest of the American economy, The Stevens found itself resurrected as a result of the Second World War and America's need to mobilize quickly to address the needs of the war effort. In December 1942, The Stevens was sold to the U.S. army for $6 million to use as classrooms and barracks for the Army Air Force Technical Training School. The military maintained the facility for less than a year before selling the hotel to an enterprising contractor and president of the Avenue Hotel Corporation named Stephen Healy. Healy set about the Herculean task of trying to restore The Stevens to some of its previous grandeur after the military occupation. Since he purchased the hotel for $ 2,250,000, a mere 20¢ on the dollar of the original price of the hotel, he thought it was worth the investment. And it soon was. In 1944, The Stevens was selected as the headquarters hotel for both the Republican and Democratic party conventions. Though the conventions were held a month apart, both parties maintained headquarters for several months at The Stevens, a mere 14 floors away from each other. The year 1944 also saw The Stevens earn another distinct honor as being the birth place of post World War II international civil aviation. From November 1 through 7, 1944, The Stevens hosted representatives of 55 governments at the international civil aviation conference that created the Provisional International Civil Aviation Organization (PIACO), which became simply the International Civil Aviation Organization subsequent to the conclusion of the war. But watching all this activity at The Stevens with increasing impatience was another shrewd investor who had his eyes on The Stevens. His name was Conrad Hilton.

The construction site of The Stevens is seen here on August 25, 1925. Chicagoans fist learned about plans for The Stevens back in 1922 when *The Economist*, in its March 3 edition, published an article under a banner headline that stated simply "15,000,000." The article told of the purchase of the Michigan Avenue property between Seventh and Eighth Streets from the Otto Young estate for $2.5 million, and the ambitious plan to build a hotel that would simply be "the largest in the world." By the time the hotel was actually built, the cost of the project was $30 million—twice the original projection.

The first steel columns arrive at The Stevens building site. The columns carried by this truck were four-feet square, 77-feet long, and weighed between 70 and 90 tons a piece. The amount of building materials used to construct the hotel was staggering. They included 18,000 tons of steel, 7,622,000 bricks, and 1,750,000 cubic feet of concrete.

Here, The Stevens is being erected in the shadow of the Benjamin Marshall-designed Blackstone Hotel, which was built and operated by the Drake brothers. The elegant Parisian-inspired Blackstone, known as "The Hotel of Presidents," opened in 1910 and played host to most of the presidents of the United States that served in the 20th century. The hotel is perhaps best known as the sight of the original "smoke filled room." During the Republican convention of 1920, a small group of powerful senators gathered to arrange the nomination of Warren G. Harding as the GOP candidate for president. The Associated Press reported that Harding had been chosen "in a smoke filled room," and a phrase synonymous with American politics was born. Regrettably, the Blackstone has been closed for several years, but the impressive edifice still stands adjacent to the Hilton Chicago.

The Stevens is starting to take shape here in this April 1926 photograph. In speaking to workers at a flag-raising ceremony at the building site in 1926, Ernest Stevens said, "Each of you have had an important part in erecting one of the most complicated and difficult structural steel jobs in the history of the building industry. . . . Nearly 20,000 tons of steel have been set, the first load of structural steel arriving on the job, Monday, November 9, 1925, just a few days less than six months ago." Out of gratitude for the hard work done so far, and as a reminder of the "part you played in the construction of the largest and finest hotel in the world," Stevens then handed each worker an envelope full of cash.

*Architect's drawing of THE STEVENS, showing the Michigan boulevard east front, the Eighth street south front, and Seventh street, separating the Stevens from The Blackstone. The frontage on Michigan avenue is 402 feet, on Seventh and Eighth Streets, each 173 feet. The building is to contain three thousand rooms. An order has been placed for four thousand beds.*

# THE STEVENS

3,000 ROOMS    *The World's Greatest Hotel*    3,000 BATHS

Michigan Boulevard, 7th Street to 8th Street, Chicago

THE Stevens Hotel will occupy the entire block on Michigan Avenue between 7th and 8th Streets—402 feet on Michigan Avenue, 173 feet on 7th Street and 8th Street.

Site covers 80,000 square feet. Building 25 stories above ground, 4 below, enclosing 20,000,000 cubic feet. 3000 outside rooms, each with private bath. Largest and finest banquet hall in the world with seating capacity for 4000 guests. Many other banquet and meeting rooms of various sizes.

Exhibition room for conventions containing over 35,000 square feet.

Across the alley, and connected with the main structure by bridges, will be a 12 story service Building fronting on Wabash Avenue.

*The Stevens Hotel is being built, is owned and will be operated by the owners of Hotel LaSalle.*

Also in April 1926, more than a year before the hotel opened, the Stevens family was already busily engaged in promoting the hotel not simply as the world's biggest hotel but as the "World's Greatest Hotel," as is evidenced by this advertisement from *The Hotel Bulletin*. The advertisement also claimed that The Stevens would possess "the largest and finest banquet hall in the world with seating capacity for 4000 guests." Undoubtedly the advertisement was referring to The Stevens's beautiful Versailles-inspired Grand Ballroom, which was an architectural marvel for its time, being completely free of pillars. However the seating capacity for the ballroom is grossly overestimated in the advertisement.

The Stevens family poses here at the grand opening of The Stevens Hotel on May 2, 1927. At the far left is Ernest Stevens, the visionary behind the hotel and his father James Stevens, who served as president of The Stevens Hotel Company. John Paul, the youngest of Ernest Stevens's four sons in the photograph, is today better known as U.S. Supreme Court Justice John Paul Stevens. The Stevens family hailed from the small Illinois town of Colchester, named for the Stevens's ancestral home of Colchester England.

A completed Stevens Hotel looks on a yet unfinished Grant Park. In a 1927 article on the hotel entitled, "A Trip through the Stevens," the architectural journalist Paul T. Gilbert wrote, "No one can predict what the changes of the next century will bring forth. It may be that today's wonder a hundred years from now will seem archaic, but the fact remains that this colossal structure . . . this masterpiece of Bedford stone, steel girders, brick, cement and marble has been built to withstand the wear and tear of ages."

The exterior of The Stevens Hotel is seen here shortly after opening in 1927. At the dedication of the hotel, Ernest Stevens stated, "Tonight, to the great city of Chicago we dedicate the realization of an ideal—the largest hotel on earth. We pledge to you that The Stevens will always provide rest, refreshment, and entertainment in such a manner and in such measure that the stranger within our gates will feel that Chicago is not only great in material things but is also host-friendly, hospitable, and kind."

Here are two views of typical guest rooms from The Stevens dating back to the hotels opening in 1927. An original Stevens's brochure stated that the hotel possessed 3,000 "home like rooms," all of which featured windows with views of the city or lake, owing to the hotels innovative design. It was calculated that if you slept in every room of The Stevens hotel for just one night, you would end up living there for more than eight years. Note that each room also had a telephone, which necessitated a staff of 75 telephone operators, more than would be required of a town of 25,000 in 1930.

Dinner in honor
of
Colonel Charles A. Lindbergh
by
The Mayor's Committee
of Chicago
and
The Chicago Association of Commerce
Saturday evening
the thirteenth of August
One thousand nine hundred and twenty-seven
The Stevens

# Presidential Election Supper

Served from 9:00 p. m. to 1:00 a. m.

## $1.00 Per Cover

❦ ❦ ❦

### M E N U

CHOICE OF

Fresh crab-meat saute, Dewey, in chafing-dish

Emince of chicken a la King, in chafing-dish

Medaillon of calf's sweetbreads with fresh mushrooms,
Virginienne, Perigourdine

Broiled sirloin steak minute, Bordelaise, Mexican

Spaghetti with chicken livers and fresh mushrooms saute,
Caruso au parmesan

Welsh Rarebit, in chafing-dish

———

French endive, orange, avocado
French or Thousand Island dressing

CHOICE OF

| | |
|---|---|
| Apple, pumpkin or mince Pie | Peppermint chocolate float |
| Cabinet pudding, wine sauce | Martha Washington layer cake |
| Grenadine sherbet | Camembert or Roquefort cheese |

Chocolate, vanilla or strawberry ice cream

———

Cafe Noir

❦ ❦ ❦

**THE STEVENS**                    *Tuesday, November 8, 1932*

Two menu covers from important dinners at The Stevens from the 1920s and 1930s are pictured here. The Grand Ballroom of The Stevens was already considered "the venue" to honor famous individuals visiting Chicago shortly after the hotel's opening. The first gala event the hotel hosted took place two days after the hotel opened, when the Motion Picture Association Ball was held on May 4, 1927. Among the 3,000 movie stars and their friends who were present for the event was the legendary director Cecil B. de Mille.

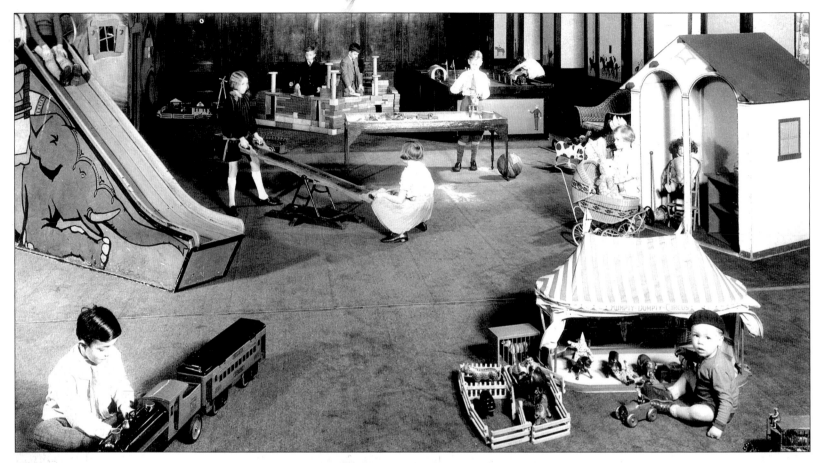

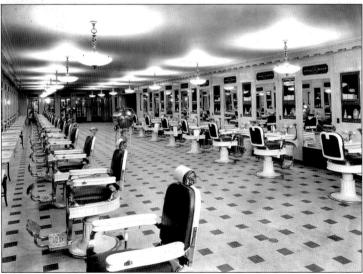

The Stevens was truly ahead of its time in offering the guests services such as the Fairyland playroom. The hotel also boasted its own hospital, consisting of two wards and an operating room, a 1,200 seat theater with "talking motion picture equipment," a five-lane bowling alley, and its own ice cream and candy factories. There was also a lending library containing thousands of volumes, and according to a Stevens brochure, "Easy chairs, good light, a view of the lake, a smoking room and an outside terrace for summer . . . to provide relaxation, entertainment and mental refreshment for the guest's free hours."

The 27-seat barber shop at The Stevens was just one of the hotel's impressive selection of amenities that allowed the guest to find all of the necessities of life and then some. Other services located at the hotel were a valet shop, a 24-hour drug store, a children's clothing and toy store, a beauty shop, a jewelry store, a haberdashery, a flower and candy shop, a newsstand, a men's manicure parlor, and a "chiropodist office" in case of foot trouble.

Pictured here is the main Dining Room of The Stevens located on the second floor of the hotel in the northeast corner facing Michigan Avenue. This site was later transformed into the Boulevard Room during the era of The Conrad Hilton. The initial order for china to supply The Stevens dining facilities was for 300,000 pieces, which came from the Scammell China Company of Trenton, New Jersey. Seven freight cars were required to ship the glassware for the hotel, which came from the Bryce Brothers plant in Pennsylvania.

One of The Stevens's most novel features was the hotel's High-Ho Golf Club located on the roof 300 feet above Michigan Avenue. The High Ho Golf Club was a full 18-hole miniature golf course built and designed by Chuck Evans. Greens fees for the course were initially 35¢ for the first round and 20¢ thereafter. A brochure touting the course stated, "powerful illumination makes night vision a pleasure." The course was open daily until 12:30 a.m. Directions to the club were simply, "Take the elevators to the roof."

The High-Ho Golf Club—Located on the Roof of the Stevens—300 Feet Above Michigan Avenue.

Here is the magnificent Grand Ballroom of the Stevens as it appeared on December 20, 1938, for the hotel's employee Christmas Party. The room is still the sight of numerous holiday parties, as well as the hotel's annual New Year's Eve party.

This is the unchanging Grand Ballroom of The Stevens at it appeared 10 years later for the 75th anniversary of the Polish Roman Catholic Union in 1948. The Grand Ballroom continues to serve as the preferred venue for the important events of Chicago's many ethnic groups such as testimonial dinners and cotillions.

The halls of the one-time Stevens Hotel now echo to the sharp whistle blasts of top sergeants and class leaders calling their men into formations. Bugles cannot be used as some classes sleep while others work. Students form into columns in the halls and move to classes in a military manner.

During the Second World War, The Stevens was taken over by the military to be used by the Army Air Force as a Technical Training School. The hotel that once comfortably hosted 3,000 guests became home to 10,000 air cadets crowded three and four to a room. Because some classes slept while others worked, the soldier-residents of The Stevens were called to formation by a whistle instead of a bugle as in the photograph above.

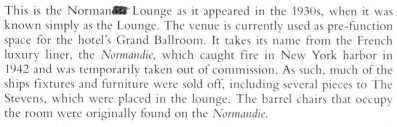

This is the Normandie Lounge as it appeared in the 1930s, when it was known simply as the Lounge. The venue is currently used as pre-function space for the hotel's Grand Ballroom. It takes its name from the French luxury liner, the *Normandie*, which caught fire in New York harbor in 1942 and was temporarily taken out of commission. As such, much of the ships fixtures and furniture were sold off, including several pieces to The Stevens, which were placed in the lounge. The barrel chairs that occupy the room were originally found on the *Normandie*.

Some of the thousands of military residents that occupied The Stevens during the Second World War are seen here. While guests of the hotel, the soldiers who were trained as mechanics, meteorologists, and instrument technicians, took their meals in the hotel's Grand Ballroom, which was converted to a mess hall. The ballroom's chandeliers were removed, and its floor was covered with linoleum as part of the transformation into a mess hall.

Seen here is the official notice presented to hotel guests by the management of The Stevens on July 13, 1942, requesting that they vacate the hotel by midnight of July 31st or before to make way for the military, which was to take over the hotel for the subsequent year.

## To Our Guests

THE STEVENS WILL BY ORDER OF THE FEDERAL COURT BE TAKEN OVER COMPLETELY BY THE ARMY ON AUGUST 1. THIS MEANS THAT ALL OCCUPANTS OF THE HOTEL WILL BE REQUIRED TO SEEK HOUSING ELSEWHERE AS OF MIDNIGHT OF JULY 31 OR BEFORE.

WE ARE INFINITELY GRATEFUL TO YOU FOR THE COMPLIMENT YOU HAVE PAID US IN OCCUPYING OUR FACILITIES, AND IT IS WITH REGRET THAT WE CONTEMPLATE THE INCONVENIENCE TO YOU.

HOWEVER, THE WAR EFFORT MUST BE SUPPORTED AND WE ARE TAKING OUR PLACE ALONGSIDE OF THOSE WHO HAVE DEFINITELY APPROPRIATED THEIR PROPERTIES TO THE GOVERNMENT.

WE EXPECT THAT WE WILL BE SEEKING YOUR PATRONAGE WHEN THE ARMY USAGE OF THE HOTEL HAS CEASED AT WHICH TIME WITH THE ASSOCIATIONS AND EXPERIENCES WE HAVE ENJOYED WITH YOU, WE WILL BE ABLE TO DO A BIGGER AND BETTER JOB.

YOURS VERY TRULY,

**THE STEVENS HOTEL**

JULY 13, 1942.                    J. A. JONES, GENERAL MANAGER

This advertisement was taken out in the *Chicago Tribune* by prominent Chicago companies in July 1943 bidding farewell to the last of the 30 classes of graduates of Chicago school's of the Army Air Force training command that were housed at both The Stevens and the Congress Hotels during the Second World War.

The Great Hall of The Stevens is decorated here for a flower show at the hotel in the late 1940s. Note that at the far end of the hall is a portrait of Conrad Hilton, which today hangs in his namesake, the Conrad Hilton Suite.

After the Second World War, the Stevens's Grand Ballroom was returned to its prewar splendor and resumed its functions as a venue for the city's most important gatherings. This photograph shows the facility being used for the convocation of 1949 Clinical Congress.

# SIX

# THE CONRAD HILTON, CHICAGO HILTON AND TOWERS, AND HILTON CHICAGO

As chapter two indicated, Conrad Hilton had long been interested in The Stevens. In *Be My Guest*, Hilton states, "I wanted the largest hotel in the world." In the late 1930s, he began purchasing mortgage bonds on The Stevens at between 20¢ and 60¢ to eventually leverage ownership. However, the army's takeover in 1942 put a bittersweet end to that. The Stevens reverted to private ownership in 1943 and was transformed back into a hotel by Stephen Healy. Hilton announced to his mother one night that he was going to Chicago on the next train and said, "I'm going to stay there until I get The Stevens." Subsequently he began negotiations with Healy that he labeled "the most nerve-wracking, bruising, and ulcer making" of his career. But in the end, Hilton purchased The Stevens for $7.5 million, netting a profit of $1.5 million for Healy.

Hilton set out to make The Stevens a flagship property in his empire, which included The Plaza, Roosevelt, Mayflower and of course The Palmer House. Amongst improvements made to the hotel was the installation of the large ice stage in the Boulevard Room supper club, which began featuring elaborate ice shows in 1948. Using his Hollywood connections, garnered partially as the ex-husband of Zsa Zsa Gabor and father-in-law to Elizabeth Taylor, he enticed celebrities to the hotel. Soon, The Stevens was frequented by such stars as Frank Sinatra, Bing Crosby, and Bob Hope.

On November 19, 1951, The Stevens was renamed The Conrad Hilton. It is still known as such by many who recall that period with fondness. It was truly a glamorous time, when the hotel played host to film stars, politicians, and royalty. In the 1950s, Bette Davis, Lauren Bacall, President Eisenhower, and Sen. John F. Kennedy visited the hotel. The most distinguished guest of the era was undoubtedly Queen Elizabeth II, who made an official visit to Chicago in 1959 for the opening of the St. Lawrence Seaway.

In the 1960s, the hotel continued its traditional role as a political headquarters, playing host to the Republican National Convention, and in 1968, acting as headquarters for the Democratic National Convention leadership. As such, it was literally center stage for the famous "Battle of Michigan Avenue," waged between anti-Vietnam war protesters and Chicago police. The Conrad Hilton opened the Hilton Center in 1962, adding a massive 75,000 feet of new function space, including the International Ballroom and the Continental Room.

By the 1970s, The Conrad Hilton was showing its age, but still drew major events because of its shear size. The Cook County Democratic Party had some of the largest dinners in recorded history, using every function room in the hotel. Towards the end of the decade, much thought was given to the future of The Conrad Hilton and consideration was given to converting it to offices or condominiums or to razing it. However, by the early 1980s, a strategic plan emerged to protect the grand Chicago hotel and to give it new life and a new name. In 1984, The Conrad Hilton closed for then the largest and most expensive ($185 million) hotel renovation ever undertaken. It was reopened on October 1, 1985, as The Chicago Hilton and Towers. The *Chicago Sun Times* trumpeted, "Hilton Reborn into Elegance" on the front page, and in another headline, stated, "Reborn Conrad Hilton again Grand Duke of Michigan Avenue."

In the following two decades, The Chicago Hilton and Towers truly reassumed its position as the "Grand Duke of Michigan Avenue." Glittering functions like the Consular Corp Ball and the Lyric Opera Ball continue to occur at the hotel, and world famous guests continue to occupy its premiere suites. New to this incarnation of the hotel are a series of annual mass-paticipation events—some of the most popular in the city, such as the annual Chicago Cubs and Chicago Bears fans' conventions and the St. Patrick's Day festivities anchored by Kitty O'Shea's Irish pub.

During the late 1980s and early 1990s, The Chicago Hilton and Towers unquestionably kept the South Loop alive during a difficult period and enabled the neighborhood to enjoy its renaissance. In 1998, in conformance with a Hilton Hotels Corporation brand initiative to place the Hilton name first, the hotel born as The Stevens, grew up as The Conrad Hilton, and reached maturity as The Chicago Hilton and Towers was re-christened as The Hilton Chicago—the name that it currently enjoys.

Today, there are few Chicagoans who have not attended some event at The Hilton Chicago. It enjoys the greatest familiarity with a wide spectrum of the city's inhabitants and truly deserves the title of "the people's palace." Perhaps of all the names that it has been called since its inception, this is the most appropriate of all.

This is an interesting photograph of members of the 1949 Clinical Congress watching television for the first time in the Normandie Lounge of The Stevens.

Conrad Hilton presides over a ceremony changing the name of the hotel from The Stevens to The Conrad Hilton. The name change was officially approved by the board of directors of Hilton Hotels Corporation on November 19, 1951, as a "tribute to the inspiration, vision, and leadership of Conrad Hilton."

Conrad Hilton greets a guest at his namesake hotel in this publicity photograph from the 1950s. In his autobiography, *Be My Guest*, Conrad Hilton stated that he had "worked hard to buy The Stevens . . . worked even harder to give her a personality, a position in the life of her city, to change her from simply the largest hotel to the largest and friendliest."

In the 1930s, The Stevens main dining room was transformed into the Boulevard Room supper club, and after the Second World War, it regained much of its splendor appearing as it did in the photograph above in 1948.

In the immediate post war years of the 1940s that began the "golden age" of supper clubs, guests like those pictured at left could enjoy two shows nightly in the Boulevard Room at 8:00 p.m. and 11:40 p.m. Dinner was $3 and up per person. Favorites on the menu at the time were Boulevard Special King Alaska Crab for $3.75 and Hollywood Style Spring Chicken for $3.85. The ever present Champagne Cocktail fetched a hefty $1.20.

Ice skaters perform in the Boulevard Room supper club of The Conrad Hilton Hotel in the early 1950s. The Boulevard Room ice shows began a 21-year run in 1948, during which time 43 original "mini musicals on skates" were performed. The Boulevard Room spawned many characters during this period, including the legendary maitre d' Phil Itta, who claimed to be the originator of the Shirley Temple cocktail—"ginger ale, some orange juice, a cherry, and a little grenadine to make it sweet."

Here is a program from one of the ice shows in the Boulevard Room of The Conrad Hilton. The ice shows were the brainchild of Hilton booking agent Merriel Abbott, who booked talent for both the Empire Room of The Palmer House and the Boulevard Room of The Conrad Hilton. She did not want the two rooms to compete directly with each other, so she conceived the idea of the ice shows for the Boulevard Room. The music and lyrics to nearly all the productions were the product of a single composer, Hessie Smith.

By the mid 1950s, the Boulevard Room had been reconfigured from a two-story venue to a one-story venue with the Williford meeting room being built on top of it. Today, the Boulevard Room, which was rehabbed in the 1984–1985 renovation, is a conveniently located meeting and banquet facility still found at the summit of the grand staircase.

Crowds wait outside The Conrad Hilton to greet Gen. Douglas MacArthur as he returned from Korea in 1951. These crowds of onlookers outside the hotel would be replicated throughout the 1950s and 1960s as a seemingly never ending parade of internationally famous guests visited The Conrad Hilton during this period.

The Great Hall of The Conrad Hilton prepared for General MacArthur to speak. Throughout the 1950s and 1960s, the Great Hall was decorated in appropriate fashion to honor various different dignitaries and heads of state who were visiting the hotel.

Chicago Mayor Richard J. Daley (left) and Conrad Hilton (right) escort Queen Elizabeth II into The Conrad Hilton in July 1959 for a dinner in her honor sponsored by the City of Chicago. Queen Elizabeth II arrived in Chicago via the Royal Yacht, which made its way down the St. Lawrence Seaway that had recently been opened.

Guests stand for the arrival of Queen Elizabeth II at the dinner held in her honor in the Grand Ballroom of The Conrad Hilton. The queen made the rounds of Chicago hotels during her less than 12 hours in Chicago. She had lunch at the Guildehall of the Ambassador West Hotel and attended a pre-dinner reception at The Drake before attending dinner at The Conrad Hilton.

This interesting diagram of The Conrad Hilton dates from the 1950s. Among its noteworthy features is the depiction of the Tower Ballroom at the top of the hotel. Today, that ballroom has been converted into the ultra luxurious Conrad Hilton Suite. Another noteworthy depiction is of the Boulevard Room supper club located to the right of the Great Hall.

This photograph of the Great Hall of The Conrad Hilton, which evokes the grandeur of the space, dates to the late 1950s. Upon seeing the Great Hall when the hotel first opened in 1927 Earle Ludgen, the veteran editor of *Hotel World*, said of the space, "I warrant you have never seen a lovelier room, not in Versailles the glorious, nor in the châteaux of southern Frances nor in the castles of Brittany."

Fashion shows have long been held in the Grand Ballroom of The Conrad Hilton, as have political luncheons. The two types of events converged on July 27, 1960, during the Republican National Convention when ladies attending the convention were treated to the Great Lady Luncheon Tableau, where heroines of American history "came alive" once again and showed the fashions of the period.

Pres. John F. Kennedy is seen exiting The Conrad Hilton Hotel with Chicago Mayor Richard J. Daley in the early 1960s when he was a frequent guest at the hotel. Some veteran Conrad Hilton waiters recall serving John F. Kennedy beer hidden in a coffee mug while he sat on the dais during the "dry" civic dinners he was compelled to attend at the hotel.

Richard Nixon speaks at The Conrad Hilton during the 1960 Republican National Convention in Chicago. The Conrad Hilton and its successors The Chicago Hilton and Towers and The Hilton Chicago has played host to every U.S. president since Harry Truman.

**INTERIOR VIEW**

A. International
   Ballroom

B. International
   Ballroom Foyer

C. Hotel Grand Ballroom

D. Continental Room

E. Continental Lobby —
   8th Street

F. Exhibition Floor

G. Hotel Exhibition Hall

*This is*

# HILTON CENTER

*The Conrad Hilton Hotel's Magnificent New Addition*

## 75,000 SQUARE FEET of NEW, SUPERB SPACE for
### Conventions • Meetings • Conferences • Exhibitions • Banquets

**EXTERIOR VIEW**

Adjacent to and connected with The Conrad Hilton Hotel, on the northeast corner of Wabash Avenue and 8th Street in downtown Chicago, the building's exterior features white precast architectural panels, is of steel structure frame with concrete floor slabs throughout entire area.

This brochure describes the new Hilton Center Convention Complex from 1962. The center cost $2.5 million to construct and featured a three-level structure containing the new International Ballroom, which was the world's largest at the time, as well as 53,000 square feet of exhibit and or meeting space. Combined with the convention facilities of the original hotel, the expanded Conrad Hilton now offered the largest convention and exhibit facilities of any hotel on earth.

This photograph clearly illustrates the scale of The Conrad Hilton's massive International Ballroom, which was built in 1962. The room was built to accommodate 4,000 for meetings and 2,600 for banquets. According to the brochure that announced its opening, the International Ballroom was "named in honor of the fine reputation Hilton Hotels have throughout the world as centers for international travelers, sites of major civic and social functions; and because of Chicago's deservingly growing reputation as an important focal point of world travel and trade."

The size of the International Ballroom enabled it to host a variety of different activities in addition to balls and meetings, which included trade shows, fashion shows, and as can be seen from this photograph, boxing, which was popular at the hotel through the 1970s.

Vice Pres. Lyndon Johnson arrives at the Conrad Hilton in 1963. He returned to the hotel as president in 1968, when before 2,200 people in The Conrad Hilton's International Ballroom, he announced that he would not be seeking re-election as president of the United States.

A smiling Prince Phillip of the United Kingdom arrives at The Conrad Hilton for a dinner in his honor in 1966 amidst the press and many spectators. Note the guests in formal wear at the top of the staircase at the entrance to the Grand Ballroom. Today, most heads of state arrive at the Hilton via the hotel's private "Presidential Walkway," which ensures security and prevents the inconveniencing of other hotel guests.

This photograph evokes much of the glamour inherent in Chicago's grand hotels: majestic architecture, elegant décor, and formally dressed guests who in this case are greeting each other in the Great Hall of The Conrad Hilton prior to attending the gala dinner in honor of Prince Phillip in 1966.

One of the most famous images of The Conrad Hilton shows military police protecting the entrance of the hotel during the notorious 1968 Democratic Convention when the "whole world watched" as the Hilton, which served as the headquarters of the Democratic Party was the focal point of ugly anti-Vietnam war protests. Hotel management went to lock the doors of the hotel to protect protesters from entering the hotel only to realize that the keys had long since disappeared because the hotel had never been locked since it was first opened in 1927.

Seen here is a photograph of the chaotic scene in the Great Hall of The Conrad Hilton during the 1968 Democratic Convention. The Normandie Lounge of the hotel, located just above the Great Hall, was transformed in to a makeshift MASH unit for the many injured protesters, police, and members of the press. It was reported that sympathizers of the protesters in the hotel hurled globs of ketchup at their colleagues on Michigan Avenue from the floors above in an attempt to get more of the "wounded" into the hotel.

Another important event for The Conrad Hilton in 1960s was the arrival of the crew of the Apollo 8 mission on January 14, 1969. Subsequent to a parade through downtown Chicago and a special meeting of the Chicago City Council, a civic luncheon was held in the Grand Ballroom of the Conrad Hilton for astronauts Frank Borman, James Lovell Jr., and William Anders. The luncheon was commemorated with both a reproduction of the Apollo 8 space capsule, as well as with appropriately festooned cakes.

This photograph dating to the late 1960s is of The Conrad Hilton looking north down Michigan Avenue. Clearly visible on the roof of the hotel are the two Imperial Suites, which were built in 1956. Designed for very special guests, the suites included floor to ceiling picture windows, a grand piano, satin sheets, a wood burning fireplace, and a personal maid. Truly, it was hospitality fit for Kings—as well as Queen Elizabeth and Presidents Truman, Eisenhower, Kennedy, Nixon, and Clinton.

Three years after the successful opening of the Haymarket Lounge, The Conrad Hilton opened the Haymarket Restaurant, which also had an old Chicago, early 1900s atmosphere. The restaurant was actually comprised of four separately-themed rooms and featured an elaborate antique carriage at the entry. The restaurant's publicity stated: "It's a place where men can eat—and eat big—that men like . . . and women like to be seen at. Plush! Fire-placed! Lavish!"

Similar to what transpired at its sister hotel, The Palmer House, the nature of entertainment at The Conrad Hilton changed during the swinging 1960s. In 1965, the hotel opened the Haymarket Lounge, which its advertising described as a "pleasure palace in a spirited turn of the century atmosphere." The advertising went on to boast that the lounge possessed "entertainment with music from the rollicking 1900s and the rocking 60s," and it also announced that drinks were available from 11:00 a.m., "served by our bouncy Haymarket Belles." One such belle is pictured in the photograph above. The lounge survived until The Conrad Hilton's 1984 renovation.

The Wine Room was one of the four distinct rooms in the Haymarket Restaurant where patrons could order such Chicago-themed specials as Hinky Dink's Planked Chopped Steak; Bathhouse John Porterhouse; "Ma" Streeter Spaghetti Milanese; and Mrs. Potter Palmer's Choice (sliced white turkey). The restaurant adopted as its motto a saying popularized from former Chicago alderman Michael "Hinky Dink" Kenna, "Chicago ain't no sissy town!"

During the 1970s, more notable visitors were feted at The Conrad Hilton. This photograph from the mid 1970s shows Mayor Richard J Daley and his wife "Sis" toasting King Carl Gustav of Sweden at a city banquet. (Laszlo L. Kondor photograph.)

The holidays are always a magical time in Chicago's grand hotels. Each of the hotels has its own holiday traditions. The Hilton Chicago continues The Conrad Hilton tradition of having an enormous Christmas tree in the Great Hall of the hotel as exemplified by this photograph taken in the 1970s. Meanwhile, The Drake builds an elaborate gingerbread village and routinely accommodates over 500 holiday shoppers a day in the hotel's Palm Court Tea Lounge between Thanksgiving and Christmas. The Palmer House has an annual holiday concert featuring nothing but tubas. The event, known as "Tuba Christmas," features over 100 tuba players and garners national media attention each year.

The Grand Ballroom of The Conrad Hilton is set for a banquet in the early 1970s. It was during this period that the hotel established a Guinness World Record for the largest number of people at one meal—7,200. The event was a fund-raiser for the Cook County Democratic Party, and it required all of the hotels' ballrooms and meeting space, as well as 480 waiters.

No, this is not a photograph of a subway station. It is actually the main corridor of The Conrad Hilton facing north in the years prior to the hotel's massive refurbishment. By the late 1970s, The Conrad Hilton had lost much of its elegance and panache and risked being completely eclipsed by a new generation of hotels that were arising in the vicinity of North Michigan Avenue. In a 1978 article, the *Chicago Sun Times* asked, "Has time passed the Conrad Hilton by?" Meanwhile, the *Chicago Tribune* in an article of the same year referred to the Hilton's lobby as "gloomy" and a "little disappointing."

The Great Hall of the Hilton is being renovated between 1984 and 1985 in this photograph. The Conrad Hilton was closed for nearly a year as the entire hotel was restored at a cost of $185 million. At the time, this was the most expensive hotel renovation ever undertaken. During the renovation, the existing 2,700 hundred guest rooms (already reduced from the original 3,000) were gutted and transformed into 1,543 larger and more elegant rooms. In the public areas, old world craftsmen painstakingly restored the 24-karat gold leaf, crystal, and marble appointments and also the original oil paintings.

No mere face lift, the 1984–1985 renovation of the Hilton literally involved rebuilding the hotel from the inside out, as this photograph illustrates. Much thought went into what to do with The Conrad Hilton in the years immediately prior to the renovation when it was losing business to newer hotels. According to a *Chicago Sun Times* article of March 29, 1984, "Consideration was given to converting it to condominium use, senior citizen housing, combined offices and apartments and demolition for complete redevelopment." Hilton had been considering building a completely new 1,800-room facility on a sight at State and Wacker, however when a proposed tax incentive for developing on the site failed to materialize, the decision was made to go forward with a complete renovation of The Conrad Hilton.

The 1984–1985 renovation afforded The Conrad Hilton the opportunity to incorporate some much needed new features into the hotel. One such feature was a seven-story 500-car parking garage, which was built adjacent to the back of the hotel. This photograph illustrates the initial stages of that construction project.

Perhaps one of the most popular results of the 1984–1985 renovation was the creation of Kitty O'Sheas Irish Pub, which is considered the granddaddy of all Irish pubs in Chicago. Many of the staff members of the pub are actually recruited in Ireland and brought here to provide the venue with added authenticity.

The Conrad Hilton reopened as The Chicago Hilton and Towers on October 1, 1985. The opening ceremony was presided over by Cook County Board Chairman George Dunne and numerous officials of the Hilton Hotels Corporation. *Lodging Magazine* termed the Conrad Hilton's renovation as the "Top Hotel Renewal of All Time" and in its July/August 1986 edition claimed to "devote an amount of space to a single hotel project (The Conrad Hilton Renovation) that is unprecedented in hotel magazine publishing."

Three legendary employees of the Hilton Chicago are pictured here: General Manager Gary Seibert, who served as general manager for over a decade between 1989 and 2000 and subsequently served as general manager of The Palmer House Hilton; the late Sam Cascio, who at age 95 was the oldest working bellman in the nation, joined The Stevens upon its opening, was employed at the hotel for the next 65 years, and started each day with a "good cup of coffee and a shot of whiskey;" and the late Noel Walsh, a 40-year-plus bellman at The Hilton Chicago who never owned a phone because "he didn't want the women to bother him."

Famed banquet waiter Don Mavar pours champagne for opera tenor Luciano Pavarotti at a Chicago Hilton and Towers party. Mavar, who retired after 50 years at the hotel, could boast serving every U.S. president from Harry Truman through Bill Clinton. "These hands," he would say proudly, "have served 10 presidents." A favorite story of Mavar's was being asked to personally serve Pres. John F. Kennedy through room service and finding the president wearing only his underwear (blue polka dot BVDs) as he brought him the order of a terrine of oyster stew and a Heineken beer.

This photograph shows the filming of the hit medical drama "E.R.," which occurs frequently at The Hilton Chicago. Few people realize that the hospital heliport viewed regularly on "E.R." is actually the roof top heliport of The Hilton Chicago. Other television series that have filmed at The Hilton Chicago include "Early Edition" and "Cupid."

Tom Hanks is seen here with Hilton Chicago General Manager Tom Loughlin during the filming of the movie *Road to Perdition* outside the hotel's Grand Ballroom. Nine major motion pictures have been filmed at The Hilton Chicago. The most famous being *The Fugitive* with Harrison Ford. Other movies that have made use of The Hilton Chicago as a filming location are *U.S. Marshals*, *My Best Friend's Wedding*, *Home Alone II*, *Primal Fear*, *The Package*, *Unconditional Love*, and *Love and Action in Chicago*. The hotel is actively marketed for the purpose of movie making because of its unique architecture and variety of filming locations.

Here is a view of the 5,000-square-foot, two-story Conrad Hilton Suite perched on the top of The Hilton Chicago. The Conrad Hilton Suite is consistently rated as Chicago's most fabulous suite. The suite sells for $6,000 per night. It has played host to Presidents Reagan, Bush (41), and Clinton, as well as to numerous foreign heads of state and other famous personalities the likes of John Travolta and John F. Kennedy Jr.

The late John F. Kennedy Junior arrives at The Hilton Chicago accompanied by his cousin William Kennedy Smith for the Physicians against Land Mines Dinner, which was held in the Grand Ballroom of the hotel.

On November 14, 2002, The Hilton Chicago celebrated its 75th anniversary with a lavish party that had as its theme the many movies that had been filmed at the hotel. The party was attended by over 400 dignitaries, including Mayor Richard M. Daley and the chairman of Hilton Hotels Corporation, Barron Hilton, pictured above, who at the culminating moment of the party took a sword to slice a piece of a giant cake in the shape of the hotel.

Pres. George W. Bush arrives to give a speech to a medical conference at The Hilton Chicago on June 11, 2003, and is escorted by General Manager Tom Loughlin. For this occasion, the presidential helicopter *Marine One* simply landed across the street from the hotel in Grant Park to facilitate his arrival to the Hilton.